Fez

City of Islam

Shaykh Mulay ᶜAlī ad-Darqāwī.

Fez
City of Islam

TITUS BURCKHARDT

Translated from the German
by William Stoddart

THE ISLAMIC TEXTS SOCIETY
CAMBRIDGE · 1992

First published in German by Urs Graf-Verlag 1960
First English edition

The Islamic Texts Society
5 Green Street, Cambridge CB2 3JU, UK

British Library Cataloguing-in-Publication Data
A catalogue record for this book
is available from the British Library

ISBN 0 946621 17 9 *cased*

Typeset by Goodfellow & Egan, Cambridge
Printed by Craft Print Pte, Singapore

Publication of this volume has been
made possible by the generous support
of Dar al-Maal al-Islami, Geneva.

ACKNOWLEDGEMENTS

All black and white photographs are the originals of the author
with the exception of p. 34, *Castle at Suntat*, by Jean Robichez.

Colour photographs with permission of the following:
pp. 98, 136, Peter Sanders Agency
pp. 6, 13, 14–15, 18, 69, 71, 72, 86, 88, 93, 99, 101, 102, 156, 161, Bruno Barbey, Magnum
pp. 10, 50, 59, 78, 94, 114, 115, H. Gruyaert, Magnum
p. 12, Steve McCurry, Magnum
p. 97, David Hurn, Magnum
pp. 8, 58, 70, 111 (both), 119, 125, Roland Michaud, John Hillelson Agency
pp. 68, 77, Sabrina Michaud, John Hillelson Agency
p. 4, Georg Gerster, John Hillelson Agency
p. 37, Didier Barrault, Robert Harding Picture Library
p. 106, Jackum Brown, Robert Harding Picture Library
p. 45, Robert Francis, Hutchison Library
pp. 120, 121, Martin Lings

Foreword

THE PUBLICATION of this book in English is like the unearthing of a great treasure which, after a brief and narrowly accessible display, had been buried with little hope of ever receiving the recognition it deserved.

Its appearance in German thirty years ago passed almost unnoticed; and what might have been a golden opportunity for it to come into its own, the World of Islam Festival in 1976, was exploited in favour of another book, one that was altogether new. Titus Burckhardt was persuaded to write his monumental *Art of Islam*, side by side with his activities as adviser to the Arts Council of Great Britain during its preparation of the unforgettable exhibition of Islamic Art at the Hayward Gallery. This and the British Library Koran exhibition may be said to have formed the crown of the Festival; but advantage was nevertheless taken of Burckhardt's unrivalled knowledge of Fez, and a few of the contents of his book came briefly to the surface at the Museum of Mankind in an exhibition accompanied by a film, both directed by him, showing glimpses, amongst other things, of craftsmen at work in the bazaars of that still exceptionally traditional city. But I will say no more here of his connections with Fez since these are the theme of the Afterword, written by an eye-witness.

Titus Burckhardt is an authority whose works are a constant source of inspiration in more than one domain. Much will therefore be expected from this new book by all those who have so long awaited its publication; and it is a pleasure, for one who has read it, to be able to assure them with confidence in advance that, to say the least, they will not be disappointed.

Martin Lings

Contents

To God belong the East and the West.
Wheresoever ye turn, there is the Face of God.
Verily God is All-embracing and All-knowing.

Koran 2:115

1 Fez

A GEODE of amethyst, brimful of thousands of tightly packed crystals and surrounded by a silver-green rim: this was Fez, the Old City of Fez, in the twilight. As we came downhill towards it, the hollow in which it lies grew visibly larger; the countless crystals, uniform in themselves, but irregularly grown into one another, now came more clearly into view; one side of them was light, while the other side, the one facing the prevailing wind, had become darkened and weather-beaten. Between them and the silver-green girdle of olive trees, the wall of the Old City with its towers could be seen. Towards the city gate now facing us—Bāb al-Gissa—the small donkey caravans made their way as of old, and from out of the gate into the evening wind and towards the expanse of green, came men and children in Moroccan dress; for it was spring, and the hills round about were covered with yellow and blue flowers.

In the heart of the city, in the lowest point of the hollow, one could make out the tent-shaped roof of green glazed tiles that covers the dome of the tomb of the holy Idrīs, the founder of Fez; nearby was a minaret. Not far away were the equally green roofs of the old Koranic college of al-Qarawiyyīn. The nearer we came to the city, the more minarets rose to Heaven, clear-cut, square, flat-topped towers, similar to the Romanesque city towers of Italy. There must have been hundreds of them. These reveal the position of the larger mosques; even more smaller mosques are hidden from sight in the confusion of the high, grey-white and, at this moment, reddish cubes of houses. A city full of sanctuaries: the European travellers who first visited it at the beginning of the century spoke either of a 'citadel of fanaticism', or marvelled at it as a place of perpetual prayer.

I asked myself whether the Old City might have inwardly changed during the twenty-five years that I had been away from it. It still looked the same as

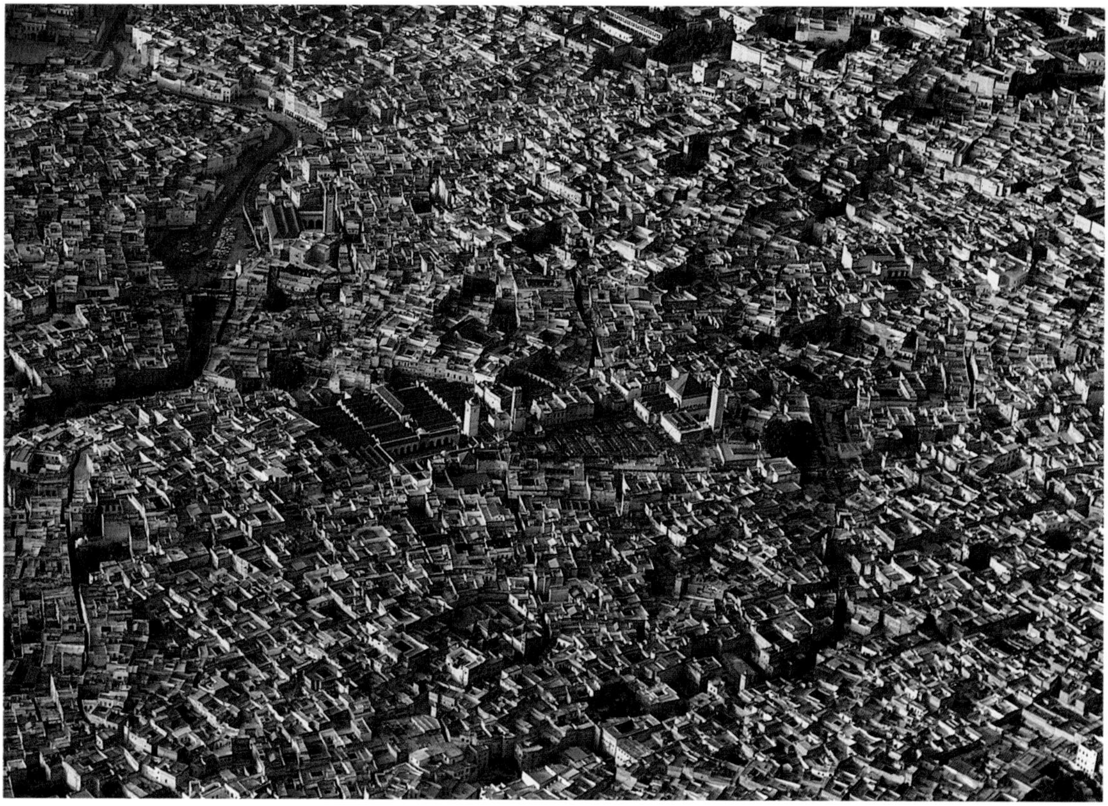

Aerial view of Fez.

before: ancient, weather-beaten, withdrawn inside its walls. Only a few groups of white houses outside in the open ground where no one had previously dared to settle, and a few miserable huts which had crept into deserted lime-pits, showed that the army of the poor had now burst outside the protection of the old walls.

On our left, towards the East, the hollow in which Fez lies opened up towards the plain of the river Sabū: a wide, flat valley on whose horizon a still snow-covered branch of the Middle Atlas, the Bū Iblān, soared. To the West, on a somewhat higher level, began the plain on which lie the medieval Sultan's city, *Fās Jadīd* 'New Fez', and further away, the modern town built by the French.

The city was getting nearer, and at the same time it loomed up within my own mind, rising out of the darkness of memory, with all of its thousand faces pressing upon me questioningly; for Fez had once been familiar to me, well known and yet full of inexhaustible secrets. In it I had experienced another world and another age, a world of the Middle Ages such as perhaps now no longer existed, an austere and yet enticing world, outwardly poor but inwardly rich. It was a city that had had to yield to foreign rule and that had accepted in silence the arrival of a new order dominated by the power of machines, yet inwardly it remained true to itself; for at the time I first knew it, men who had spent their youth in an unaltered traditional world were still the heads of families. For many of them, the spirit which had once created the Mosque at Córdoba and the Alhambra at Granada was nearer and more real than all the innovations that European rule had brought with it. Since then, however, a new generation had arisen, one which from its earliest childhood must have been blinded by the glare of European might and which in large measure had attended French schools and thus henceforth bore within it the sting of an almost insuperable contradiction. For how could there be any reconciliation between the inherited traditional life which, despite all its frugalities, carried within it the treasure of an eternal meaning, and the modern European world which, as it so palpably demonstrates, is a force entirely orientated towards *this* world, towards possessions and enjoyments, and in every way contemptuous of the sacred? These splendid men of the now dying generation whom I had once known had indeed been conquered outwardly, but inwardly they had remained free; the younger generation, on the other hand, had won an outward victory when Morocco gained political independence some years ago, but now ran the grave risk of succumbing inwardly. It was thus not without some anxiety that I returned to the familiar city, for nothing could be more painful than the sight of a people robbed of its best inheritance, in exchange for money, haste and dissipation.

In front of the city gate there was still the neglected cemetery with its irregular crop of graves between mule tracks and flowering thistles, where children were playing on white slabs and, here and there, men sat silently waiting for sunset and the call to prayer.

Just then the last pink glow on the towers disappeared. The sun had completely set and now only the green-gold of the sky shed a mild, non-shadow-forming light, in which everything seemed to float as if weightless and somehow glowing in itself. At that moment the long-drawn-out call to the sunset prayer rang out from the minarets. Lights appeared in the towers. But the city was silent; only a few cries, like suddenly broken-off laments, reached our ears. The wind which had suddenly arisen and which, high above us in the town, blew from mountain to valley, interrupted the sound. But the people who were waiting had heard the call. One could see both individuals and groups spread out their prayer mats and turn towards the south-east, the direction of Mecca. Others hurried through the city gate to reach a mosque, and it was with the latter that we ourselves entered the city.

We were immediately enveloped in the half-light of the narrow streets which descended steeply from the various gates into the hollow where the great sanctuaries lie surrounded by the bazaars or commercial streets (*aswāq*; sing. *sūq*). In the streets all that can be seen of the houses are the high walls, darkened with age, and almost entirely without windows. The only open doors are those of the *fanādīq* (sing. *funduq*) or caravanserais, where peasants and Bedouins visiting the town leave their steeds and beasts of burden, in

open spaces surrounding a courtyard, and where, on the upper storey, they can hire a room to pass the night or store their wares. Otherwise the street is like a deep, half-dark ravine which turns unexpectedly, sometimes here, sometimes there, often covered in by bridges from one building to another and only wide enough to allow two mules to squeeze past each other. Everywhere the cry *Bālek*! *Bālek*! ('Take care! Take care!') rings out. Thus do the mule drivers and the porters with heavy loads on their heads make their way through the crowd. Only further down do the shops begin, where the traveller on arrival may find his necessities; there too are the saddlers, the basket-makers and the cookshop-owners, the latter preparing hearty meals on little charcoal fires. We proceeded past them into the street of the spice-dealers (*Sūq al-ᶜAṭṭārīn*), which runs through the entire town centre, and in which one shop lies hard against the next, a row of simple plain boxes, with shuttered doors in front, just as in Europe in the Middle Ages, and with no more space than will allow the merchant to sit down amongst his piled-up wares.

Nothing stirs the memory more than smells; nothing so effectively brings back the past. Here indeed was Fez: the scent of cedar wood and fresh olives, the dry, dusty smell of heaped-up corn, the pungent smell of freshly tanned leather, and finally, in the *Sūq al-ᶜAṭṭārīn*, the medley of all the perfumes of the Orient—for here are on sale all the spices that once were brought by merchants from India to Europe as the most precious of merchandise. And every now and again one would suddenly become aware of the sweet smell of sandalwood incense, wafted from the inside of one of the mosques.

Equally unmistakable are the sounds; I could find my way blindfold by the clatter of hooves on the steep pavings; by the monotonous cry of the beggars who squat in the dead corners of the streets; and by the silvery sound of the little bells, with which the water-carriers announce their presence when, wending their way through the *sūqs*, they offer water to the thirsty.

But now I paid attention only to the faces, which here and there loomed up in the glimmer of the newly lit lamps; I thought perhaps to recognise an old friend or acquaintance. But I saw only the features of familiar racial types: sometimes grave and worthy figures, sometimes the sly and slightly scornful townsman, but no known face. There were also youths, dressed more or less in the European manner, with the mark of a new age on their foreheads, and sometimes staring defiantly and inquisitively at the foreigner.

To the right of the spice market, just beside the Sepulchral Mosque of Idrīs II, the holy founder of Fez, there is a cluster of narrow passages lined with booths. Here all kinds of clothing are on sale: coloured leather shoes, ladies' dresses in silk brocade embroidered in gold and silver. Near the mosque there are also decorated liturgical candles, frankincense and perfumed oils; for perfumes belong to the *sunna*, the sacred Tradition, according to the saying of the Prophet: 'Three things from your world have been made worthy of my love: women, perfumes, and the solace of my eyes in prayer.'

FAR LEFT:
View from the hills to the North of Fez; within the high, centuries-old, mudbrick walls, rise the green roof and minaret of the sepulchral mosque of Mulay Idris II.

Around the Sepulchral Mosque of the holy Idrīs there is a narrow alley, made inaccessible to horses and mules by means of beams. This constitutes the limits of the *ḥurm*, the sacratum, within which formerly no one might be pursued. Only a short time before the French withdrawal was this rule broken for the first time—in the revolt against the French-imposed Sultan Ben ᶜArafa.

We walked along the arabesque-decorated outer walls of the sanctuary, past the little window, covered with an iron grille, which opens on to the tomb, and reached another brightly lit street which brought us into the vicinity of the great mosque and college of al-Qarawiyyīn. In the streets surrounding it the advocates and notaries have their little offices and the booksellers and bookbinders have their shops—just like their Christian colleagues of old in the

The Spice Market, Sūq al-ᶜAṭṭārīn.

shade of the great cathedrals. As we passed by, we stole a glance through several of the many doors of the mosque and gazed into the illuminated forest of pillars, from which the rhythmical chanting of Koranic *suras* could be heard.

Then through the district of the coppersmiths, where the hammers were already at rest and only here and there a busy craftsman still polished and examined a vessel in the light of his hanging lamp; soon we reached the bridges in the hollow of the town and ascended from there to the gate on the other side, the Bāb al-Futūḥ. As we looked back we saw the Old City lying beneath us like a shimmering seam of quartz. I now knew that the face of Fez, the old once-familiar and yet foreign Fez, was unaltered. But did its soul live on as formerly?

On one of the following evenings we were invited home by a Moroccan friend, to a house which, like all Moorish houses, opened only onto an inner courtyard, entirely white, where roses grew in profusion and an orange tree sparkled festively with blossoms and fruits. The room on the ground floor, where the guests sat in threes and fours on low divans, opened onto this courtyard. Amongst all the men present, there was also a small dark-skinned Arab boy, whose thin face was as if transfigured by an inward fire as well as by a child-like smile. The master of the house told us he was the best singer of spiritual songs in the whole country. After the meal he invited him to sing to us. The boy shut his eyes and began, softly at first, and then gradually more loudly, to render a *qaṣīda*, a symbolical love-song. And some of the guests who had gathered near him and had drawn back the hoods of their *jellabas* sang the refrain, which contained the *shahāda* (the attestation of Divine Unity) in a harsh, ancient Andalusian style. The Arabic verses of the poem grew faster and faster, in a quick, intense tempo, while the answering refrain surged forth in widely extending waves. All of a sudden the volume of the chorus, which until then had only 'answered' the singer, flowed on without interruption and branched into several parallel rhythms, above which the voice of the leading singer continued at a higher pitch, like a heavenly exultation above a song of war.

It was miraculous how the many strands of the melody never came together in those accords which allow the flow of feeling to rest as if on a broad couch and which promise to human longing an all too easy, all too human consolation; the melody never turned into a worldly 'space', its different strands never came together as if reconciled; they continued endlessly, circling undiminishingly around a silent centre, which became ever more clearly audible, as a timeless presence, an other-worldly 'space', without yesterday or tomorrow, a crystalline 'now', in which all impatience is extinguished.

This was Fez, unalterable, indestructible Fez.

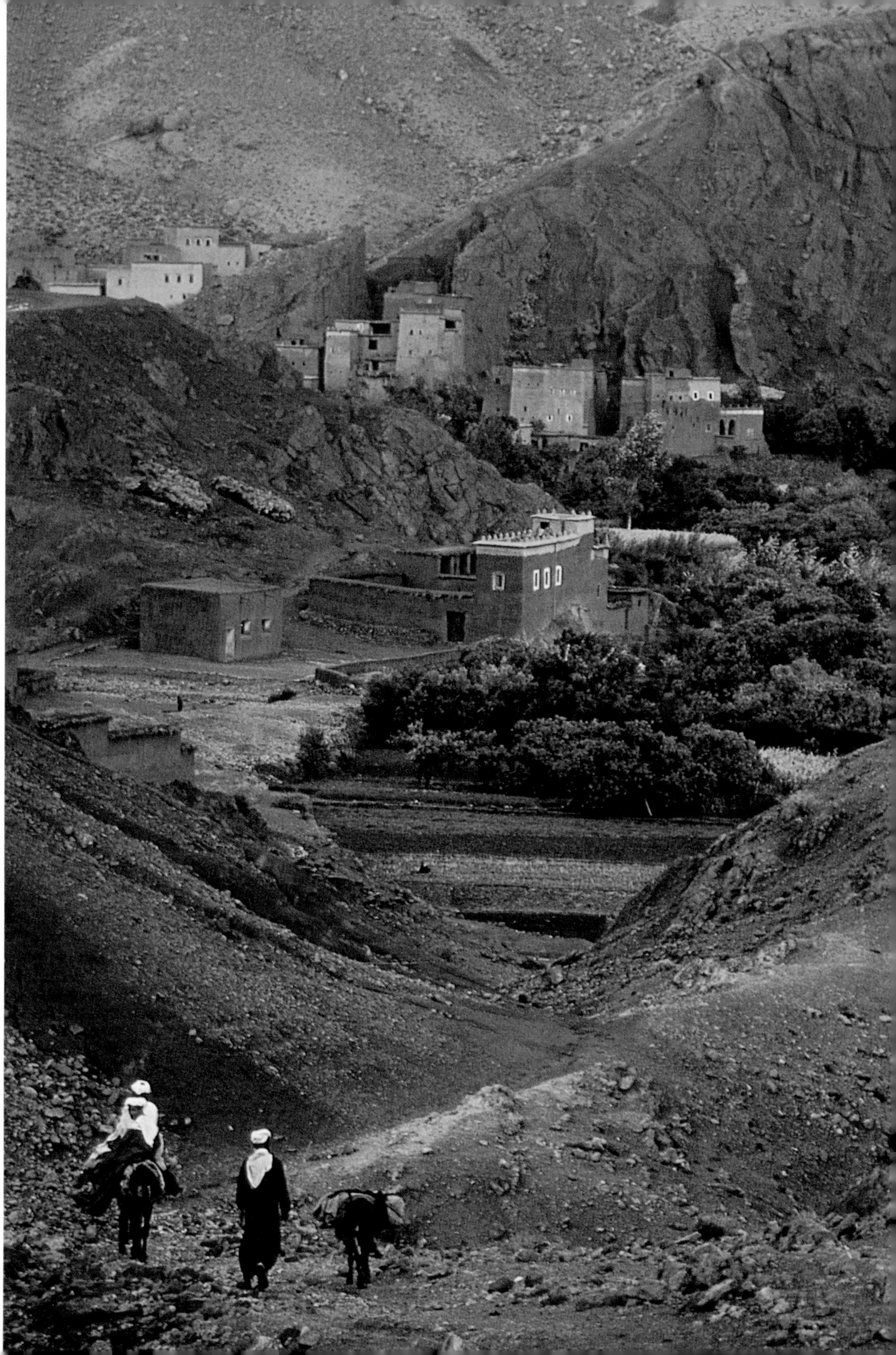

2 City & Desert

ACCORDING to Ibn Khaldūn, the great Arab historian who lived and taught in Fez from 1354 to 1363, the political destiny of all the peoples that live between the Mediterranean and the great deserts of further Asia, Arabia and Africa, is governed by the opposition between nomads and sedentaries. The desert is the unchanging kingdom of the wandering herdsmen who, because of their hard struggle for existence, always remain at the beginning, so that their original abilities, courage, alertness, and sense of community never wane. Any surplus population that the desert cannot feed constantly gravitates to the fertile areas, in the middle of which are the towns. The city is the most perfect expression of the sedentary form of life and the natural goal of all culture, for there alone can science, art and trade reach their full development; at the same time however, it is the place where human society begins to decay, so that sooner or later towns fall prey to nomadic conquerors. And so all the movements of peoples that have led to the founding of states and empires originated in the desert and declined in the town.

This law holds good especially for that part of North Africa that runs from Syrtis Minor to the Atlantic coast. The Arabs call this the 'West' or 'Occident' (*al-Maghrib*)—'the land of the setting sun' and the part of this which coincides with contemporary Morocco, is called the 'Far West' (*al-Maghrib al-'aqṣā*). This area is distinguished from the 'eastern' and 'central' Maghrib in that its fertile and almost completely flat interior is cut off from both the Sahara and the Mediterranean; for, to the north, a wall is formed by the Rif mountains, which for almost the entire length of the coastline descend steeply to the sea, while, to the south, the Middle and High Atlas ranges shelter the country from the far-flung desert. It is only along the Muluya valley, which separates Morocco from Algeria, that the Sahara desert almost reaches the north coast. This tongue

FAR LEFT: *Berber village in the Atlas Mountains.*

Nomad tents on the edge of the Sahara.

of the desert constitutes the Tāza Gate, through which from the earliest times waves of nomads streamed into the Moroccan heartland, the Gharb. Less often they came from the south, over the passes of the Middle and High Atlas mountains. In the West, the plain of the Gharb runs along the Atlantic coast, where for a long time it was protected from invaders from the sea, not by a ridge of mountains, but by a coastal sandbank. Up until the modern age navigation here was restricted to a very few estuaries. Between the two seas lie the foothills of Tangier. These form a natural bridgehead to the easily visible Spanish coast.

Before the spread of Islam, the whole of Maghrib was almost exclusively populated by Berbers. It was only in the seventh century that the Arabs advanced from the east and, bringing with them Islamic culture, settled chiefly in the cities. Somewhat later, towards the tenth century, Arab Bedouins also expanded towards the Saharan regions and even to the northern plain, thus causing the Berbers to retreat more and more to the mountains and, in smaller groups, to as far away as the Atlantic ocean.

The Berbers belong to the Hamites, a branch of the white race, to which the Fulba, the Hausa, the Galla and the Somalis also belong. Their language, which has many features in common with ancient Egyptian, and whose characteristic and rather hissing sound can be heard in such place-names as Tazenakht,

Taurirt, Azru, Tilghemt and Sheshawen, lives on in the dialects of the individual tribes, despite the presence of Arabic, which under Islam was universally introduced as the literary language.

OVERLEAF: *Berber village near Ouarzazate.*

Since in Morocco there is every possible transition from Saharan waste to fertile, agricultural country, there is also to be found here every possible way of life, from pure nomadism to sedentarism. Ibn Khaldūn, who in his 'Introduction to the Science of History' (*Muqaddima*) classifies the various populations according to their ways of life, designates all who dwell in the open country as 'Bedouins', that is to say, inhabitants of the *bādiya* or desert. By this he means not only the desert of sand or stone, but all areas which lie outside the fortified oases and the town holdings, and which are protected neither by walls nor by a standing militia. In North Africa, in fact, the desert or 'steppe' in which the nomads and semi-nomads wander often extends right up to the walls of the towns. Even in the fertile area of the Gharb, in the neighbourhood of Fez and Meknes, one need only ride for three hours in order to reach the black tents of the wandering herdsmen. And thus immediately next to centres of city culture are to be found people whose way of life has scarcely altered for millennia or at least since the time of Abraham. Outside the vicinity of the town most of the

The village of Tinerhir glows in the rays of the setting sun.

land until recently belonged not to individual owners, but to tribes or clans, irrespective of whether the land was for cultivation or merely for pasture. In this way even the agricultural sedentaries, the *fellāḥīn*, are closer to nomadism than are the farmers of Europe. Their frugal villages, built of sun-dried brick bearing speckles of the surrounding arable land, lie scattered in the sea of the steppe, looking like so many islands menaced by the tide of the nomadic tribes.

> The inhabitants of the desert, writes Ibn Khaldūn, live naturally, that is to say from agriculture or cattle-breeding. As regards nourishment, clothing, and the other necessities of life, they content themselves with only the essential. Luxury is unknown to them. For their dwellings they use tents made of hair or wool, or wooden huts, or houses made of mud or stone. These are not adorned with any furniture, since they are only intended for shelter and refuge. Sometimes they live in caves. Their food receives little or no preparation or, at most, is prepared on an open fire.
>
> Those who sow grain and other crops are sedentaries. They include the inhabitants of the small settlements and villages, and also the mountain dwellers. They constitute the great mass of the Berbers and non-Arabs. (*Muqaddima* 2:2)

Such is the way of life of the Berber Kabyles and of the Jebāla in the Rif mountains in the north of Morocco. Their small widely-scattered villages are covered with gabled straw roofs to cope with the rain which, because of the proximity of the sea, is heavier here than inland. Hedges of fig-cactus protect the farms from wild animals and enclose the herds at night. Wheat and oats thrive on the flatter slopes, where the dark bushes of the dwarf palms have been planted, and olive trees grow alongside the rivulets in the valleys.

In the High Atlas and in the valleys which on its southern side descend toward the Sahara are large fortified towns, with high towers at their four corners, built of sun-dried mud bricks. Their tapered walls, crowned with crenellated battlements, are curiously reminiscent of the buildings of ancient Mesopotamia. Probably here, in these remote protuberances of the desert, a very old building style has been preserved, a style which once extended over wide areas of the Near East and North Africa and whose furthest extensions are to be found in the south of Arabia. The Moorish influence has not essentially changed this architectural style; it has merely enriched the square and step-ladder decorations, which are ingrained on the mud walls, with a few extra designs. It may well be therefore that these intrepid Berber strongholds still look the same as in the time of Sumer and Assyria, or as in ancient Canaan; at any rate neither the wide landscape, in whose red expanse the sparse fields border the river like green or golden carpets, nor the strong figures of the Berbers with their simple cloaks and turbans wound round their heads like wreaths of flowers, in any way contradict this picture of an ancient and timelessly enduring world.

> The Bedouins, who live by breeding animals such as sheep and cattle, mostly wander hither and thither to find pasture and drinking water for their herds. They are known as shepherds and cowherds. They do not penetrate deeply into the desert, since there they would not find enough grass. People of this kind are (in the West) the Berbers and (in the East) the Turks, and also the Turcomans and Slavs who are related to them.
> (*Muqaddima* 2:2)

These shepherds and cowherds lead a semi-nomadic life since, depending on the season, they either camp with their flocks or else live in their mud-brick and stone villages. They are to be found on the higher levels of the Middle Atlas.

In a few regions where the rock is soft, the permanent dwellings of the Berbers are cavities hewn out of the mountainside. A slanting passage with steps leads down to a central room, in the roof of which a round hole opens on to the mountainside, in such a way that the smoke from the fire can escape and some light from outside can get in. Smaller excavations surround this central space, like rooms around a patio or like the choir and transepts of an early medieval church. Sheepskins are strewn on the floor, earthenware jugs are kept in small recesses, and in niches in the walls are beds of twigs and skins. This is the oldest way of life amongst the Atlas peoples, and it may indeed be the heritage of an archaic culture, which some scholars think was a matriarchal one, in which woman, as defender of the species, and the earth, as mother of all living things, played a central role.

Amongst the Berbers of the Atlas it is not the custom of the women to veil their faces. Their dress is beautiful in its simplicity: a single seamless cloth is wrapped around the body, fixed on both shoulders by large silver brooches, and gathered up at the waist by a broad girdle. A scarf whose fringes hang over the temples and merge with the silver and amber jewelry adorning the neck, holds in place a headdress of wool. In cold weather the Berber women put woollen blankets with embroidered borders round their shoulders, and wear coloured knitted trousers.

On the western slopes of the Middle Atlas and the southern slopes of the High Atlas the shepherds and cowherds meet the camel breeders who come up from the Sahara. Of the latter Ibn Khaldūn says:

> Those Bedouins who eke out a living from camel breeding penetrate more deeply into the desert, as the hillside pastures of grass and bushes do not provide the right feeding for camels; for these animals must eat the shrubs of the desert, drink its salty water and, in winter, find refuge in the

warm desert air. In the desert sands there are also protected places where they can give birth to their young. No animal has more difficulty in giving birth than the camel and for this reason it needs the heat. Consequently, the camel breeders have to live deep in the desert's interior. Often they are driven by the militia from the mountains into the desert and indeed they flee there in order to avoid the fines and reparations demanded from them on account of their incursions. This is why they are the wildest kind of people. Compared with sedentary people, they are like beasts of prey. In the west (i.e. in the west of the Islamic world, the Maghrib) certain Berber tribes belong to this category, as do, in the east, the Kurds, the Turcomans, and the Turks. But the nomadic Arabs advance yet further into the desert: they are even more closely bound to it, for they live exclusively from camel breeding, whereas other groups keep sheep and cattle as well as camels. Consequently the nomadic Arabs represent a group of people who are conditioned by nature and who of necessity belong to human society . . . (*Muqaddima* 2:2)

The Arab Bedouins who migrated to Morocco during the Middle Ages brought the desert with them.

It is remarkable, writes Ibn Khaldūn, that in all the places that were conquered by the Arab Bedouins, culture disintegrated, settlements were deserted and even the earth was destroyed. The Yemen, where the Arab Bedouins live, has apart from a few towns become a wasteland. Likewise in Arab Iraq, Persian culture has been completely destroyed. The same is true for Syria. When at the beginning of the fifth century (i.e. eleventh century A.D.) the Banū Hilāl and the Banū Sulaym overflowed into Ifriqiya (Tunisia) and the Maghrib, and waged war there for three hundred and fifty years, they took possession of the flat land with the result that the plains of the Maghrib were entirely laid waste. Previously the whole area between the Sudan and the Mediterranean was settled, as the remains of monuments, sculpture and the ruins of villages and hamlets prove . . .

The Arab Bedouins are a wild people . . . Their wildness is dear to them, for it means for them freedom and independence from all authority . . . All the activities of the Arab Bedouins are connected with travel and movement. This is the exact opposite of sedentary existence which alone gives rise to culture. When, for example, these Bedouins need stones on which to place their cooking utensils, they pull down some abandoned building in order to obtain them. If they need wood for their tent-poles, they tear down a roof . . .

It is their way to prey on everything that other people possess. Their

FAR LEFT: *Dades Valley in the snow-covered slopes of the High Atlas.*

halting place is wherever the shadow of their lances falls . . .
(*Muqaddima* 2:25)

But Arab nomadism does not merely have a barbaric, anti-sedentary, aspect; it also possesses a certain warlike nobility, which the famous Emir ʿAbd al-Qādir, that bold and skilful warrior who opposed the French invasion of Algeria at the beginning of the last century, celebrated in his poems:

O thou who preferrest the dull life of the town
to wide, free solitude,
dost thou despise nomadic tents
because they are light, not heavy
like houses of stone and lime?
If only thou knewest the desert's secret!
But ignorance is the cause of all evil.
If thou couldst but awake in the dawning Sahara
and set forth on this carpet of pearls,
where flowers of all colours shower delight
and perfume on our way.
We breathe an air that lengthens life,
because it ne'er blew on the refuse of towns!
If at dawn, after the night's dew,
thou wouldst from a high point look into the distance,
thou wouldst see on the measureless horizon
fallow beasts grazing on scented meadows.
At a moment like this all care would leave thee
and rest would enter thy restless heart.
On the day of decampment the camels' *howdahs*
are like anemones weighed down by rain.
They cover virgins, who peep out through peepholes.
Ah peephole which the eye of the *houri* fills!
Behind them sing the drivers in high pitch,
their song more gripping than flutes and cymbals.
But we, on noble horses
whose decorations cover breast and croup,
stir ourselves into a gallop.
We hunt gazelles and beasts of prey.
None can outrun our rapid coursing!
At night we return to the tribe
which has already encamped on an unspotted site.
The earth is like musk; even purer it is;
and generous too, moistened at dawn and dusk by rain.
There we put up our tents in rows.

The Earth is dotted with them as the sky with stars.
Those who have passed on truly said
—and truth undergoeth not change—
beauty is found in two things,
in a verse and in a tent of skin.
When our camels graze at night,
their lowing resounds like the thunder of early morning.
They are the ships of the desert; whoso travels
on them is saved, but how dangerous are the ships of the sea!
They are our mehari, swift as antelopes,
through them and our horses we achieve fame.
Our horses are always saddled for battle;
whoever seeks our aid, for him we are ready.
For fame we have sold our citizenship forever,
for fame is not won in the town!
We are kings! None can compare himself with us!
Does he then truly live, who lives in shame?

(*ʿAbd al-Qādir*)

LEFT BELOW:
A Berber from the Middle Atlas.

BELOW:
Arab nomads from the Muluya Valley.

Berber horsemen at a festival.

The Arab Bedouins who reached Morocco remained pure camel breeders only in the south, on the edge of the Sahara and in the Muluya valley, near the border with Algeria. In the plain of the Gharb, they became to a certain extent mixed with the Berbers already settled there, especially the warlike, semi-nomadic and horse-riding Zenātā, and gradually adopted their way of life; they reared cattle, cultivated the land in places, and built villages, but without ever completely giving up their nomadic tents. Even today, in their frugal settlements, the black tent, now used for the women's quarters, stands in an enclosure of thorns close to the characteristic round straw hut or lower room of sun-dried brick, the whole giving an appearance of flotsam from the steppes; it is as if the Arab Bedouins had only hesitantly and temporarily adopted the peasants' way of life.

While the Arab nomadic tribes in the north thus gradually became sedentary, the Sanhājā-Berbers to the south of the High Atlas adopted at an early stage the way of life of the camel breeders. In their wanderings over the Sahara they got as far as Senegal, which takes its name from them.

These are the several varieties of the 'Bedouins' of whom Ibn Khaldūn speaks.

CULTURE AND CIVILIZATION

According to the criteria implied by the European word 'civilization', all these nomads and semi-nomads would be deemed to be rougher, duller and less mannered than city dwellers; for 'civilization' means precisely the development of cities. The ideal which in Europe lies behind this concept goes back to the Romans, for whom the whole Roman Empire was merely a prolongation of their *civitas*, their city-state. This is expressed visibly in the axial cross, in the form of which the Romans laid out all their settlements, and which had the effect of extending these far beyond the limits of their cities and hamlets, in such a way that all inhabitable land was drawn into its clear order: this is the expression of a static world view, the realization of a regulated and measurable cosmos, in which man was supposed to feel at home. The Christian Church—and also a few Muslim philosophers of the Middle Ages—adopted this concept of culture as an all-inclusive city, but more in a figurative than in a literal sense. Only the European Renaissance, and *a fortiori* French rationalism, which found its expression in the French revolution, adopted completely literally the 'civilization' of man as its goal. Not for nothing do all Frenchmen call themselves 'citizens': members of the *civitas* of France. And so also as colonizers in North Africa, the French presented themselves as the true successors to the Romans: Rome had once set foot in that country; Arab nomadism, the French alleged, had merely interrupted a development which, for the good of North Africa, must be recommenced and continued. The nomads must be subdued, brought under a strong administration, and gradually settled.

According to Ibn Khaldūn, on the other hand, the perfect condition of human society does not find its peak in the one-sided development of sedentary life, but in a balance between nomadism and sedentarism. This ideal is not merely fashioned by the nature of those countries which, without a certain amount of uncultivated wilderness, would quickly succumb to the never-ceasing encroachment of the sand, just as today similarly placed inland plains in North America are threatened; it also corresponds to the spiritual attitude of Islam: the masculine and combative virtue which Islam favours, finds a natural basis in nomadism. The constant awareness of the ephemerality of everything on earth, that constitutes its life's breath—*everything perisheth save His Countenance*, says the Koran—is like a sublimation and a spiritual reinterpretation of the experience of the nomad, the wandering herdsman, who neither sows nor reaps, neither builds nor sculpts, and never stays permanently anywhere. On the other hand, however, the sacred prototypes of Mecca, Medina and Jerusalem accord to the city in Islam a spiritual meaning; its heart is the mosque, with its saints and scholars. Through the mosque the city becomes a kind of crystallized revelation of the Intellect.

The city is indeed a crystal, not only in terms of meaning but also in its form: in the double aspect of perfection and immobility, both of which herald death. In order that the city may not die or inwardly decay, it must be continually nourished by the influx of nomadic elements while, contrariwise, the Bedouins must share in the spiritual influence that emanates from the city. Should this equilibrium be impaired, the city culture is either suffocated by spiritual inbreeding or overrun by nomads. 'Consequently the Bedouins are the origin of all social order amongst the sedentary peoples and in the towns . . .' The civic condition, however, can only mark an endpoint; 'it is the last step in cultural development and thereby the point at which culture begins to decay. It is also the last step in decadence and in separation from the original good . . .'

> In its natural and primordial condition, the soul is ready to receive everything, good or bad, that comes its way, and to form itself therefrom. The Prophet said: 'Every child is born in the primordial condition. It is its parents who make it a Jew, a Christian or a fire-worshipper'. To the extent that the soul, from its beginning, is influenced either by one quality or the other, that is to say either by good or by evil, it continues in the same direction, and later finds it difficult to revert to the opposite quality . . . Sedentary people, for their part, are busy with all sorts of enjoyments. They are used to luxury and success, and to giving in to their worldly desires. Consequently their souls are coloured by every kind of reprehensible and negative characteristic. The more they possess, the further removed they are from the ways and manners of goodness. Sometimes they lose all restraints. Some of them, in their gatherings, and even in the presence of their elders and in the company of women, love to conduct unseemly conversation. They have no sense of reticence, dominated as they are by their bad habit of being publicly dissolute in word and deed . . . (*Muqaddima* 2:3)

In the case of the Bedouins, on the contrary, virility and dignity are inborn; they are the mark of their freedom; this contrasts sharply with the bumpkin-like quality widely attributed to the European peasant since the time of Cervantes and Brueghel, and which in the last analysis derives from serfdom. Ibn Khaldūn does not idealize the nomad; he knows his hard and sensual nature; if the townsman is hungry for enjoyment,

> the Bedouin can be just as worldly. Only, his worldliness concerns the bare necessities of life and not luxury or anything else that stimulates artificial desires and provides enjoyment. Thus the morals that the

> Bedouins observe in their dealings with one another are good; compared with the sedentaries, their bad habits and characteristics are much fewer . . . They are thus more responsive to right guidance than are the sedentaries.
>
> Sedentary people are used to cowardice and softness. They are sunk in good living and luxury. They delegate the defence of their life and property to the sovereign who rules over them and to professional soldiers whose function is to protect them. Within their walls and fortresses they feel safe. No noise arouses fear in them, and no chase ever takes away their breath. They are careless, and have lost the habit of carrying arms. Generation after generation has grown up in this way of life, and they have thus become like women and children who are dependent on the master of the house. Eventually this becomes second nature, and replaces the natural disposition of man . . .
>
> The Bedouins, on the contrary, live apart from society. They live alone in open country and without the protection of professional soldiers. They have neither walls nor gates. Therefore they defend themselves and do not rely on the protection of others; they always carry their weapons with them, carefully look in all directions, and allow themselves but little sleep—when they are together in sufficient numbers—or else sleep in the saddle. They hear every distant barking, every slightest stir. They penetrate the desert alone, relying on their own strength. Virility has become part of their being, and courage their very nature . . .

Laws are admittedly necessary, but

> when respect for laws is enforced by punishment, this gradually destroys all virility; for when one punishes someone who cannot defend himself, one humiliates him and breaks his spirit . . . state and educational laws destroy virility, for their compulsion comes from outside. This is not so in the case of the laws of faith, whose dominion is inward. Thus the influence of state and school on sedentary people is to make their souls weak and non-resistant . . . (*Muqaddima* 2:4–9)

The quality of leadership thus comes from the Bedouins. For 'leadership depends on qualitative superiority, and this derives only from tribal consciousness.' This is proper to the Bedouins, for

> only tribes possessed of a strong consciousness of solidarity can exist in the desert . . . Their camps are usually defended by a standing body of warriors composed of the noblest young men of the tribe. The protection afforded to the settlement by these warriors is all the stronger, the more

> they are united to one another by common descent. Family competitiveness strengthens their character and makes them feared by their enemies for only blood relatives are always ready to face death for one another. (*Muqaddima* 2:2)

Thus consciousness of the purity of their descent is a further characteristic of the Bedouins. But this is an aristocratic characteristic, a natural prerequisite for the founding of princely houses and dynasties.

Another law of desert life is allegiance, the cohesion of a group under a leader: 'In the Bedouin tribes all discipline and direction come from the elders, the shaykhs; they usually enjoy considerable respect amongst their people . . .' The allegiance of a tribe to its leader however is something quite different from servility; the shaykh is obeyed because he is the head of a large family or because he is courageous and wise, and successful in his deeds. It is expected of him that, before taking important decisions, he consult with the elders of the other families of the tribe. This chivalrous conception of leadership also obtained when the Sultan, as legal head of the state, invested the shaykh with a public office, which always occurred when the ruler sought to ensure the loyalty of a tribe. The report of a French diplomat who, in 1886, as ambassador for his government, rode from Tangier to Fez, lets us see this state of affairs as clearly as if it were in a mirror:

> . . . Towards ten o'clock in the morning we arrived at the place of Shaykh Mubārak of the Aulād Delīm and erected our camp opposite his house, on a hill completely covered with marigolds that were fluttering in the morning breeze. In front of us rose the first hills of the Zerhūn range, where the founder of the Moroccan empire, the famous Mulay Idrīs found his first refuge. Round about us, as far as the eye could see, there stretched out other high mountains, without trees and apparently without villages, so that their creviced ridges were completely bare. They looked like enormous waves that had suddenly frozen under the hand of Allāh. This impression was strengthened by the reflection on their flat surfaces of the bluish colour of the sky. Here and there this was broken by large white cracks in the chalky ground that resembled flecks of foam in a powerful ocean. The house of Shaykh Mubārak lay in the valley at the foot of the hill on which was our camp. Compared with the size of the neighbouring villages, the space occupied by his house indicated clearly that it was the abode of a lord, a citadel filled with vassals, a meeting place, and the seat of the power dominating the region. This impression was strengthened further when, in the afternoon, we went to visit the *caïd*. Firstly we were taken to an Arab courtyard, in the middle of which a fountain played. The courtyard served as a stable; the horses of the bodyguard stood there in the open with their forelegs bound. In the corners all sorts of baggage was

> heaped up. A few women washed clothes at the fountain, while others were weaving in a sort of hall. Servants ran hither and thither; there was a life and a bustle that bore witness to the presence of a large number of people. We were not to visit the whole building, however, which apart from the women's quarters contained enough apartments to lodge a hundred warriors. We were taken up to the reception room, which was composed of two long chambers linked to each other by elegant arches. One of these chambers was used by the servants; in the other, along the walls of which cushions had been placed for our use, Shaykh Mubārak sat on a low divan. The odour of fever that met us as we entered the room amply proved that it was not for lack of goodwill that the old Shaykh had not met us on horseback at the border of his land. One felt this all the more on seeing the Shaykh himself. Although aged, he was still erect, and would have been handsome if the fever had not ravaged him. His yellow skin was in stark contrast with the whiteness of his turban and his beard. His eyes shone brightly, but this was not the effect of the fever . . . As soon as we sat down, we were brought all kinds of food on large platters, while a dignified member of the household began to prepare tea with all the well-known ceremony. But our attention was caught even more by the arrival of a group of riders who seemed to have returned from some mission. Each of them approached the Shaykh, making first of all a bow, and then bending down to kiss his knee. The Shaykh put his hand paternally on the shoulder or forehead of each of them, and spoke a few words as the one concerned remained in this inclined position. All this took place, however, without any crass servility, but rather with a simplicity that was redolent of greatness. This homage to the tribal chief had nothing demeaning about it, as one could clearly see from the free and affectionate manner in which they later spoke with the Shaykh. One after another they again stood up, went into the neighbouring room, and sat down together on the carpet. (*Charmes*)

By their very nature the Bedouins are opposed to absolute overlordship.

> Nevertheless, when a man who has attained the rank of leader on the basis of tribal consciousness sees the way to true lordship opening up before him, he follows this way, for the goal in sight is a desirable one. It can only be reached, however, on the basis of tribal consciousness, for this alone assures him of allegiance. Thus kingship is the goal to which tribal consciousness ultimately leads . . . (*Muqaddima* 2:16)

For Ibn Khaldūn kingship is the form of government that springs from nature, and thus is willed by God. For kingly dignity is something prefigured in the essence of man. It represents in a sense the summit of earthly existence, since it permits the development of all the faculties and demands the exercise of all the virile virtues. If this rank is attained only by a few, its realization is nevertheless like the manifestation of a prototype which every man carries within himself, so that the subjects of a king see in him as it were the fulfilment of their own essence.

Ibn Khaldūn considers no form of government other than monarchy, and his judgement on this matter would undoubtedly have been the same as that of the famous Emir ʿAbd al-Qādir who, during his captivity in France, learned that King Louis-Philippe had been replaced by a 'Council of the Republic' composed of five members: 'But to be effective a body must have a head,' he remarked to the French officer who had brought him the news. 'It will not have one head, but five!' the latter replied. To which ʿAbd al-Qādir exclaimed: 'I tell you: it will not have five heads, but thirty-two million, and that is a little too many!'

If the city cultures repeatedly, or periodically, succumb to the onslaught of nomads or semi-nomads from the 'desert', this does not necessarily mean that the Bedouins will destroy the city culture. The Bedouin conquerors may do violence to the town-dwellers, but they let town life go on and merely assume the lordship of it as an aristocratic governing class which in fact becomes gradually absorbed by it. According to Ibn Khaldūn this process of assimilation is unavoidable:

> Within a given ruling family leadership exhausts itself after four generations: the originator of the family's fame knows what efforts his work has cost him and therefore preserves those qualities that were the foundation of his power. The son who inherits his authority has had a personal relationship with his father and has learned from him . . . The third generation however contents itself with an outward imitation of its predecessors and relies on custom . . . And finally the fourth generation no longer possesses any proper idea of the effort that went into the creation of the authority. It believes that deference is due to it merely on account of its noble descent . . . (*Muqaddima* 2:14)

And so begin both the transformation of the aristocratic stratum into a city officialdom and the decline of the ruling house.

The weakness of the Berbers lies in their very strength, in the exclusivism of tribal consciousness that makes one tribe the enemy of another. For this reason, as Ibn Khaldūn observes, a Bedouin movement can only create a large state when the demands for supremacy springing from the various tribes are subordinated to a leadership of a higher order, and this can only be prophethood or a function deriving from it. In this encounter between a power gushing forth naturally from the timeless sea of the desert and a Truth of supernatural origin lies the whole destiny of the Islamic peoples. The epic beginning was destined to repeat itself periodically even if on a lesser scale: the beginning when the disunited desert tribes, mostly nomadic and scarcely noticed by the surrounding civilized cultures, were united by the message of the Koran, became the vehicle of a spiritual mission, and suddenly conquered and transformed the whole near-eastern world from the Indus to the Pyrenees. As the power of the Arabs became absorbed by the urban cultures, other nomadic peoples, like the Turks and Mongols in the east and the Berbers in the west, assumed the role of the ethnically and spiritually renewing power that had succeeded in shattering the petrifications of the cities.

ISLAM

The first wave of the Islamic expansion burst through north-west Africa all too quickly; its impetus thrust on as far as Spain, carrying with it a horde of Berbers. Andalusia was like a large oasis where the nomadic onrush found its rest and where the new faith was able to develop its potential as regards science and arts. In comparison with this, the Islamic princedoms in the Berbers' own country appeared merely provincial. Even the theocratic monarchy that had been founded in northern Morocco towards 800 by a descendant of the Prophet named Mulay Idrīs was unable to assert itself over a sedentary population still under the remote influence of the Roman heritage, and actually became spiritually dependent on the Andalusian caliphate as well as on centres of Islamic culture further east.

It was only when the Andalusian culture, having become as it were over-rich, degenerated into a multitude of petty princedoms, that a wave of warlike nomads, in the middle of the eleventh century, erupted from the Sahara. These were the Almoravids who in the name of a moral renewal and a stricter and purer application of the Koranic law, conquered the whole of Morocco, the greater part of Algeria, and Muslim Spain, and transformed them into a single empire.

THE ALMORAVIDS

These warlike nomads were the Lamtūna, a tribe of the camel-breeding Sanhājā. They were called the 'veiled ones' for their men, like the Tuareg to whom they are racially related covered their faces, while their women remained unveiled. 'Almoravid' is the Spanish form of the Arabic *al-murābiṭūn* 'the people of the *ribāṭ*' for their movement originated in a *ribāṭ*, or castle of a kind of military-monastic order dedicated to fighting for the faith, which had been founded by a theologian called ᶜAbdallāh ben Yasīn on an island off the coast of Senegal far to the south. *Murābiṭ* has entered the French language as *marabout*.

The first result of ᶜAbdallāh ben Yāsīn's activity was the conversion of the Berber nomads of the Sahara, who had accepted Islam only very superficially. After he had educated, in his *ribāṭ*, an elite of tribal leaders and turned them into loyal disciples and followers, he undertook the task of subduing with the sword all the unruly desert tribes. This was successful, and, because of its increasing strength, the movement which he had launched, unexpectedly turned north, towards the oases at the foot of the Atlas, whence it finally burst forth into the fertile midlands.

As a leader ᶜAbdallāh ben Yāsīn was just, but severe, which as a leader of sons of the desert he had to be. A particular incident characterizes him: he had nominated his disciple Abū Bakr, a tribal chieftain, as commander of the Almoravid army. One day he said to Abū Bakr: 'Thou hast committed a fault, and I must punish thee for it.' 'What have I done?' asked Abū Bakr. 'I shall tell thee that later. Prepare thyself.' The disciple bared his back and ᶜAbdallāh gave him ten blows with a leather thong; thereupon he said: 'In battle thou exposest thyself too much to danger. The leader of the army must not allow himself to come to harm, for should he fall, this is a severe set-back for his troops.'

ᶜAbdallāh ben Yāsīn fell himself in 1058 in battle against the heretical Berghwātā in the Atlantic plain north of the Atlas. Abū Bakr took over the leadership of the Almoravids in his place.

For the conquest of northern Morocco, which was almost completely inhabited by sedentary people, the Lamtūna had need of a political experience and prudence which as nomads they did not have. This came to them however in the shape of a clever woman of city origin:

> . . . After his conquest of Luata (north of the Middle Atlas) Abū Bakr returned to Aghmat (at the foot of the High Atlas) where he had previously married a woman named Zaynab, the daughter of Isḥāq al-Huwārī, a merchant from Kairuan. She was strong-willed, shrewd, prudent and judicious and so skilled in business that she had been given the nickname 'sorceress'. The Emir remained three months with her, until an emissary from the south brought him the news that the Sahara was in a state of tumult. Abū Bakr was a pious and temperate man who could not suffer that Muslims should be attacked, and their blood unnecessarily shed. He thus resolved to travel to the Sahara himself, in order to restore order and repulse the unbelievers from the Sudan. On the day of his departure he took leave of his wife in the following words: 'O Zaynab! Thou art a creature of great goodness and perfect beauty; but I must leave thee and go to the Sahara, there to seek the reward of martyrdom in the holy war. As a frail woman, thou couldst not bear to follow me and live in the desert. Therefore I divorce thee. When the legal delay is over, thou shouldst marry my cousin Yūsuf ben Tashfīn, for he is my lieutenant in the Maghrib.'
>
> After he had thus separated from Zaynab, the Emir rode off from Aghmat and traversed the Tadla until he reached Sijīlmāsā in the Sūs, where he remained a few days to organize the government. Before he left this town, he called his cousin Yūsuf ben Tāshfīn to him and named him prince of the Maghrib. He gave him full power and commanded him to

wage war on what remained of the Maghrāwā, the Banū Ifren, the Kabyles, the Zenātā and other hostile Berbers. The leaders of the Almoravids recognized Yūsuf as supreme head, since they knew that he was pious, virtuous, brave, decisive, enterprising, strong, and moreover, just. He therefore proceeded to penetrate into the Maghrib with half of the Almoravid army, while the Emir Abū Bakr pushed towards the Sahara with the other half. This took place in the month of Dhu'l-qaʿda 433 (1061 A.D.). Yūsuf ben Tashfīn married Zaynab, the skilful adviser, and thanks to her political sense, he succeeded in subduing most of the Maghrib.

The Emir Abū Bakr was successful in pacifying the rebels in the Sahara and in ridding the country of them. Thereupon he assembled a large army and moved towards the Sudan, which he completely subdued, in spite of the fact that the country is so large that it takes three months to cross it. Yūsuf ben Tashfīn, for his part, conquered most of the cities in the Maghrib and consolidated his power. When Abū Bakr heard how great his cousin's empire had become, he left the Sahara and set out to thank him and take over from him. But Yūsuf, who guessed his intention, asked his wife Zaynab for advice. 'Thy cousin Abū Bakr', she said, 'is a pious man, who does not like shedding blood. When thou meetest him, refrain from showing him the honour which he is accustomed to receiving from thee. Show him neither courtesy nor humility, but receive him as one who is thine equal. At the same time bring him precious gifts such as materials, clothing, provisions and useful and rare objects. Give to him richly, for in the Sahara everything that comes from here is rare and costly.' Yūsuf followed her advice; as the Emir Abū Bakr approached Yūsuf's territory, Yūsuf came out towards him, and greeted him abruptly without dismounting from his horse. The Emir, who had observed Yūsuf's retinue, was astonished at its size, and asked: 'Yūsuf, what does this army mean?' 'It is to serve me against whosoever may be ill-intentioned towards me', he replied. This answer and the greeting from horseback aroused Abū Bakr's suspicion, but seeing also the thousand heavily laden camels approach him, he asked: 'And what is this caravan for?' To which his cousin replied: 'O Prince, I have come to meet thee with all that I possess by way of treasures, materials, clothing, and provisions, so that thou lackest for nothing in the Sahara'. On hearing these words the Emir understood all, and said: 'O Yūsuf, come down from thy horse, and hear my counsel'. So both dismounted, a carpet was spread out for them, and they sat down. The Emir began: 'O Yūsuf, I gave thee the power, and God will hold me responsible. Therefore fear God and think on Him in all thy dealings with the faithful. May thy good deeds assure me freedom in the world to come, and assure this likewise to thyself. Watch carefully over the needs of thy subjects, for God will call

> thee to account for this. May God Most High perfect thee. May He afford thee His aid and lead thee on the right path, in justice towards thy people; for He is now my attorney towards thee and all thy subjects.' Thereupon he returned to the Sahara and spent his life waging war on the infidel, until finally, in the year 480 (1087 A.D.), he was struck by a poisoned arrow, and achieved martyrdom, after he had extended his empire across the whole Sahara, as far as the Jabal Dhahab (the Mountains of Gold) in the Sudan. And the whole of this empire was inherited by Yūsuf ben Tashfīn. . . (*Rawḍ al-Qirṭās*)

As capital of the empire Yūsuf ben Tashfīn founded in 1062 the city of Marrakesh, on the northern edge of the High Atlas, at the point where the more important passes cross to the Sahara. In imitation of the oases of the Sahara, he surrounded the city with an artificially irrigated palm-grove. It is from the

A tribal chief and his horsemen accompanied by musicians on their way to a festive gathering.

Spanish form of Marrakesh—Marruecos—that is derived the name Morocco which is now used to designate the whole of the 'Far West'. In 1063 Yūsuf moved to Fez, the erstwhile capital of the Idrisids. In the west, he extended his rule as far as Tangier, and in the east, as far as Algeria, and accepted from the Abbasid Caliphs in Baghdad the title 'Commander of the Faithful' *Amīr al-mu'minīn*. When Alphonsus VI of Castile invaded Andalusia, Yūsuf responded to the appeal of the Spanish Muslims, took his army across to Spain, and destroyed the Christian forces at Badajoz in 1086. In so doing he also conquered Andalusia for himself and his heirs.

The rule of the Almoravids favoured the extension of Andalusian culture into the country of the Berbers. It created peace and well-being. Nevertheless the dynasty of the Almoravids suffered the same fate as that ascribed by Ibn Khaldūn to all ruling houses of nomadic origin: it became urbanized; the tribal consciousness of its aristocratic stratum was weakened, and its moral mission, the renewal of the Koranic legislation, finally became the exclusive affair of professional scholars and officials.

THE ALMOHADS

And thus, some eighty years later, in 1130, a second, and even more powerful wave of Bedouin Berbers, burst into North West Africa and Andalusia. This time the movement came in the form of the semi-nomadic tribes of the High Atlas, the Masmūda; they called themselves *al-muwaḥḥidūn*, 'the testifiers of (Divine) Unity', which via Spanish has become 'Almohads'. The mission of the Almohads had a deeper content and a wider application than that of the Almoravids. In contrast to their literal and outward interpretation of the Koran, which had encouraged an all too human conception of God and a merely quantitative notion of Divine Oneness, Ibn Tūmart, the spiritual founder of the Almohads proclaimed a metaphysical interpretation of *Tawḥīd*, the Koranic doctrine of Oneness, according to which God is one, not merely in terms of number, like one thing amongst many, but in His very Essence; He is unique, because there is nothing that can be compared with Him. In his commentary of *Tawḥīd* in the Berber language Ibn Tūmart writes:

> There is no God apart from Him to whom all existence points, and regarding whom all creatures testify that He is absolute and infinite, free from all determination by time, space, direction, boundary, kind, form, shape, measure, relationship or state. He is the First which nothing follows, the Last which nothing precedes. He is unique, without being anywhere, sublime, without being anyhow, lovable, without being like anything. The mind cannot picture Him, thoughts cannot reach Him, reason cannot describe Him . . . He is free from ignorance and constraint, free from impotence and need. His is greatness and majesty, glory and perfection, knowledge and choice, lordship and power. To Him are life and eternity, and to Him belong the most beautiful Names. He is one in His beginninglessness. In Him there is nothing but He Himself, there is

A Berber citadel (kasba) at Suntat in the Atlas mountains.

> no existence apart from Him, neither earth nor Heaven, neither water nor air, neither emptiness nor fullness, no light and no darkness, no night and no day, nothing living and nothing sentient . . .

for in the sight of the Infinite, whatever is finite is nothing.

This adamantine teaching, free from all representation, was both the message and the battle-cry of the Almohads; for, according to their conviction, all those who called themselves believers but thought of God as an anthropomorphic being endowed with various faculties, were no better than heathens: their literal unitarianism, which placed God on the same level as differentiated things, was unwitting polytheism, and therefore the very error that the Koran seeks to oppose.

In a visit to the eastern Muslim world, Ibn Tūmart had become familiar with the teachings of the great theologian Al-Ashᶜarī and the scholar and mystic Al-Ghazālī. On returning to the Maghrib he began to criticize the ways of the Almoravids and to attack the scholars whom they approved, until he was persecuted and had to flee with his followers into the High Atlas, to the tribe of the Masmūda, who were hostile to the Lamtūna, and over whom, by his preaching, by politics, and later also by violence, he acquired an enormous influence. He led an ascetic life. In support of his role as leader, he had recourse to the mystical tradition, widely accepted by the Shiites, according to which, in all ages, a spiritual heir of the Prophet would preserve the doctrine in all its purity. The Masmūda saw in him the *Mahdī*, the 'rightly-guided one', of whom the Prophet had said that he would renew Islam towards the end of time.

In the unassailable high valley of Tinmal on the Wādī Nafīs, the power of the Almohads grew as if in a reservoir, and finally burst forth with irresistible force and overflowed into the whole of the Maghrib.

Ibn Tūmart did not himself live to see the overthrow of the Almoravid empire. His gifted disciple ᶜAbd al-Mu'min, who later took the title of Caliph, carried out the task. With his men from the hills he crossed the successive Atlas chains, passed in a large curve through Tāza, reached the mountains in the

Map of Morocco.

north of the country, and finally, accompanied by an overwhelming number of allied tribes, moved down to the plain to win the battle against the cavalry of the last Almoravid sultan. The new empire which he created comprised the countries which are today known as Morocco, Algeria and Tunisia, and also finally Andalusia, which he plucked from the advancing Christian armies.

> The Emir ᶜAbd al-Mu'min ruled with wisdom and goodness. He excelled over all the Almohads in his virtue, knowledge, piety and horsemanship. The colour of his skin was white, and his cheeks were reddish; he had dark eyes, a tall stature, long and fine eyebrows, an eagle-nose and a thick beard. He was fluent in speech, familiar with the sayings of the Prophet, well-read and indeed learned in the things of the faith and of the world, and a master of grammar and history. His morals were beyond reproach

> and his judgement sound. He was a generous warrior, enterprising and imposing, strong and victorious . Thanks to God's help he never attacked a country without capturing it, nor an army without vanquishing it. He was particularly fond of men of letters and scholars, and was himself a good poet.
>
> It is related that he once rode out in the early morning with his minister Abū Ja^cfar ben ^cAtya, in order to spend the day in one of his gardens near Marrakesh, when from the street he espied behind a lattice window the face of a young woman as beautiful as the sun. His eyes met the eyes of the maiden, and he uttered the verse: 'The sight of this lattice and this face has pierced my heart; O virgin of Paradise, who could see thee and remain unenchanted?' But Abū Ja^cfar replied to him in verse: 'Banish this passion from thy heart, it is unworthy of the man who is the victorious sword of the Almohads.' At these words the Emir joyfully thanked his minister and rode on . . .
>
> ^cAbd al-Mu'min was as infallible in his judgement as he was powerful. He was so modest that he gave the impression that he possessed nothing. He liked neither diversions nor distractions and never rested. The whole of the Maghrib was subject to him, and Spain fell into his hands; from the Christians he took Mehdia in Africa and Almeria, Evora, Baeza, and Badajoz in Andalusia . . .
>
> (*Rawḍ al-Qirṭās*)

In 1195, near Alarcos, his successor Ya^cqūb al-Manṣūr so decisively defeated the Christian army that was trying to reconquer Andalusia, that Moorish domination in Spain seemed assured for the foreseeable future.

The century of the Almohads was for the Maghrib the blossom-time of mysticism and of the philosophy related to it. The Almohads' public support for the writings of Al-Ghazālī, which up till then had been condemned and banned in the Maghrib, had far-reaching effects that even influenced Christian scholasticism. By expounding the symbolical character of all revelation, Al-Ghazālī overcame once and for all the dangerous dichotomy between the purely literal interpretation of the Koran and its philosophical (and virtually rationalistic) interpretation. And in so doing, he opened the way for a general recognition of mystical wisdom—Sufism—from whose riches he had drawn his teachings.

It was under the Almohads that Maghribi art received its characteristic stamp. Like the Cistercians, who in the same century were spreading the Gothic style in Europe, they insisted that there be a purification of art, that it be divested of all worldly excesses; and they did this with a full awareness that it was in keeping with their rigorous doctrine of Divine Unity. In this simplification and essentialization of art forms there was also a Berber influence, and

The prayer-niche of the Almohad mosque at Tinmal, built by the Caliph Yaᶜqūb al-Mansūr over the grave of Ibn Tūmart.

this, together with the Arab-Andalusian heritage, gave rise to that perfect style which, in reference to the ancient Mauretania where the Berbers lived, is called Moorish.

An apparently unimportant, but in reality highly significant, act of the Almohad caliphs was the issuing of a new coinage which was square in shape instead of round. This was meant to symbolize the end of the historical cycle, and the founding of a definitive and lasting order.

But even the Almohads had to undergo the fate of all the Bedouin dynasties. What finally took the edge off their swords was not a diminution of their military might but a weakening of their rather one-sided faith in the mission of their *mahdī*. Not only did the majority of scholars in the land remain tacitly opposed to the innovations in the law; at the court itself, where philosophers like Ibn Ṭufayl and Averroes (Ibn Rushd) were frequently present, a new spirit was awakening.

According to Averroes it is not possible to expound and unveil the highest metaphysical meaning of revelation in such a way as to make it equally clear and obligatory for every human being. Man's capacity to understand varies according to the individual. Most people can only grasp the literal meaning of a holy scripture; others remain attached to visual and as it were mythological imaginings; and only a few are capable of penetrating its deeper meaning:

> When one expounds the deeper meaning of the Scriptures to someone without innate understanding, one leads him and oneself into infidelity. For in order to uncover the deeper meaning of the words, one must in a sense destroy the literal meaning. If one does this in front of someone who can only grasp the outward meaning, and thus without there being a possibility of opening this person's mind to a wider understanding, then one drives him, where the fundamentals of the sacred law are concerned, towards unbelief . . . (*Averroes*)

The unitive doctrine of the Almohads was thus too divested of a visual and literal character to be able to speak to the mass of the faithful. At the same time, in its own way, it could lead to a spiritual limitation. It was doubtless with this in mind that the great mystic Muḥyi'd-dīn ibn ʿArabī, who lived in Fez from 1194 to 1196, could write:

> The unilateral affirmation of Divine Transcendence leads finally to a limitation of Divine Reality. The one who denies all comparability in regard to God and who insists exclusively on this point is either ignorant or pretentious. The representative of exoteric knowledge who unilaterally emphasizes the transcendence of God, without at the same time mentioning His Immanence, is unconsciously imputing lies to God and His messengers; while fully believing that he is hitting the target, he is in

> reality far from so doing, for he is behaving like one who accepts one part of the revelation and rejects another . . .
>
> For God reveals Himself in every being in a particular manner and in conformity with this being . . .
>
> Likewise whoever compares God to something without at the same time affirming His incomparability, attributes limits to Him and does not recognize Him. Only he who, in his knowledge, synthesizes the two points of view of incomparability and of analogy . . . really knows Him, even if only in a global manner . . . (*Fusūs*)

The Almohad dynasty ruled for approximately one hundred years. In the first half of the thirteenth century, their power in Spain began to waver; in 1212 the Almohads were defeated by the Christians at Las Navas de Tolosa; the eastern provinces of the Maghrib fell out of their hands, while the Merinids (Banū Merīn), a nomadic tribe of the Zenātā Berbers, swept into the Gharb from southern Algeria through the Tāza gap.

Before their final defeat, however, the Almohads themselves had destroyed the basis of their power:

> The Emir of the Faithful, Idrīs al-Ma'mūn ben Yaᶜqūb al-Manṣūr ben Yūsuf ben ᶜAbd al-Mu'min, known as Abū'l-ᶜUlā or al-Ma'mūn . . . had an excellent knowledge of the sciences, of the Arabic language, of politics and of history. He was author of several outstanding works, was well-versed in the commentaries . . . and at the same time energetic, inflexible, despotic, ready to undertake great things, and unhesitating and cruel in meting out judgement. He was born in Málaga in 581 (1184/85 A.D.). No sooner was he caliph than the whole country was in flames; everywhere there was war, rebellion, shortages, famine, and insecurity on the roads. The enemy overran the greater part of the Muslim lands of Andalusia, while the Hafsids conquered Ifriqiya (Tunisia) and the Merinids, advancing into the Maghrib, gained control of many territories and entrusted their government to their relatives and friends; the position was such that people no longer knew to whom they owed allegiance. It was as in the words of the proverb: 'The deer appeared in such numbers that the dogs no longer knew which ones to chase'. (*Rawḍ al-Qirṭās*)
>
> The first proclamation of al-Ma'mūn as caliph took place in Seville on Thursday the 2nd of Shawwāl 625 (1227 A.D.), and all provinces of Andalusia, as well as Tangier and Ceuta across the straits, recognized him. Immediately afterwards he sent a message to the Almohads in Marrakesh to accept his rule and to overturn his brother al-ᶜĀdil. His orders were immediately carried out; al-ᶜĀdil was murdered; the tribal

shaykhs pledged their allegiance to al-Ma'mūn and had the *khuṭba* (sermon) in the mosque delivered in his name. But later they changed their minds, because of the fear which al-Ma'mūn inspired in them, and on the same evening they proclaimed his nephew Yaḥyā as caliph. Abū'l-ᶜUlā (al-Ma'mūn) received the document of his recognition by the Almohads of Marrakesh in Seville, and had it published throughout Andalusia. Thereupon he left for Algeciras, whence to embark for Morocco. But at Algeciras he heard the news that the Almohads of Marrakesh had deserted him in favour of his nephew Yaḥyā. Thrown into a rage, he quoted the words uttered by Ḥasan on the death of the Caliph Othman: 'Hear ye the cries arising from their houses? Come forward, men, and hasten to avenge Othman!' He sent a messenger to the King of Castile and requested his help against the Almohads in the form of a Christian army that would cross with him to Morocco. The King of Castile replied 'I will give thee the army that thou requestest on condition that thou hand over to me ten fortified places on the borders of my territory which I myself shall select. In addition, if God help thee and thou reach Marrakesh, thou shalt build a Christian church in that city, where the soldiers who have accompanied thee, can worship God, and where bells will announce their times of Prayer. Should any Christian convert to Islam, thou shalt not accept him, but shalt hand him over to his brothers, who will judge him according to their laws; but should any Muslim wish to become a Christian, no one must hinder him.'

Since al-Ma'mūn accepted these conditions the King of Castile sent him a proud army of twelve thousand Christian horsemen, who were to serve him and cross to Morocco with him . . . This army reached him in the month of Ramaḍān 626 (1228 A.D.) and left immediately for Morocco.

But scarcely had al-Ma'mūn departed, when Andalusia rose up, and most of its provinces proclaimed the sovereignty of Ben Hūd, the prince of eastern Spain.

In the meantime, al-Ma'mūn had embarked at Algeciras and landed in Ceuta in the month of Dhū'l-qaᶜda. After staying for a few days in this fortified place, he set out for Marrakesh, in the vicinity of which, on Saturday the 25th of Rabiᶜ al-awwāl 627 (1229 A.D.) at the time of the afternoon prayer, he came up against Yaḥyā with the army of the Almohads. Yaḥya was defeated and fled into the mountains. The majority of his soldiers were killed, and al-Ma'mūn entered Marrakesh, where he was recognized as ruler of all the Almohads. He himself mounted the pulpit in the mosque of Al-Manṣūr, and after he had delivered the sermon to the people, he cursed the Mahdī and his deeds: 'O ye men!' he exclaimed, 'say no longer that the Mahdī is sinless (*maᶜṣūm*), but that he is a deceiver (*maḍmūm*), for there is no *Mahdī* (i.e. renewer of the divine order who comes towards the end of the cycle) except Jesus, son of Mary, on whom be peace! I say to you that the whole story of your *Mahdī* is nothing but lies and deception!' And at the end he added: 'O my Almohad companions! Do not think that I have said this merely to keep the sovereignty with which you have entrusted me. Whoever it be that will succeed me will tell you the same, if God wills.' Thereupon he descended from the pulpit and immediately despatched proclamations to all the countries subject to his command, in which he invited the people to turn away from the *Mahdī* and from all the innovations that he had introduced to the Almohads. He commanded that the name of the *Mahdī* no longer be mentioned in the Friday sermon and that the gold and copper coins which he had minted be declared invalid. He ordered that the square coins of the *Mahdī* be made round, and he had it proclaimed that anyone henceforth using the square coins would be guilty of heresy. Then he returned to his palace and for three days no one could see him. On the fourth day, he ordered all the Almohad shaykhs to come to him, and when they had assembled, he said to them: 'O Almohad companions! You have incited riots and rebellions, and have gone far in your iniquity; you have betrayed the trust that was put in you, you have betrayed the lawful authority, you have killed my brothers and my uncles, without a thought for the benefits they had heaped upon you.' Producing the letter of submission that they had sent him in Seville, he showed it to them as proof of their treason, and they struck their hands as a sign of their confusion and shame. But Al-Ma'mūn turned to the judge (*qāḍī*) al-Makkāwī, whom he had brought with him from Seville, and said: 'What is thine opinion, O doctor; what is to be done with these traitors?' The judge answered: 'O Commander of the Faithful, God Most High, in His revealed Book has said: 'Whoever violates his oath, violates it to his own detriment; and whoever remains faithful to his oath, God will give him an immense reward!' The Emir replied: 'That is indeed God's truth, and according to it they must be judged, for those who do not judge according to the Book are truly guilty.' He then condemned to death all the shaykhs and nobles of the Almohads, and they were executed to the last, along with their fathers and their children. Meanwhile there was brought to him the young son of his sister who was scarcely thirteen years old and who could already recite the Koran by heart. When the boy saw how close he was to death, he said: 'O Commander of the Faithful, show mercy to me because of three things'. 'What are these,' asked the Emir. The child replied: 'My youth, my relationship to thee, and my knowledge of the Holy Book!' The Emir saw the judge and asked of him: 'What dost thou think of the plea of this creature?' The judge answered: 'O Emir, it is written: if thou leave them alive, they would only deceive your servants and breed impious and faithless people.' Thereupon the Emir let them kill his young nephew. Then he ordered that the severed heads be exposed on the walls of the city, and there were so many that the whole wall encircling the city was covered with them . . .

THE MERINIDS

But already a new wave of nomads was bursting into the 'Far West':

The Banū Merīn lived in an area that extended southwards from the Zab to Sijīlmāsā. They were nomads, and circulated amongst the Berbers in the desert. They knew neither money nor coins and were not subject to any prince. Proud and disdainful by nature, they brooked neither attack nor alliance. They knew nothing of agriculture or commerce and occupied themselves exclusively with hunting, horse-breeding and raiding. Their possessions consisted of horses, camels and black slaves. They nourished themselves on meat, fruits, milk and honey. A host of them came every summer to the West to pasture and water their horses. In autumn they would gather together at Agerṣif and from there return to their region. That was their custom for as long as could be remembered. In 613 (1216 A.D.) they came as usual to the West, and discovered that everything there was in uproar. They heard that the (Almohad) army had been defeated in the battle of ʿUqāb (Las Navas de Tolosa) and found everywhere deserted places frequented only by lions and jackals. And so they established themselves in the deserted country and immediately informed their brethren of the new situation: 'Come and join us here', they said to them, 'there is pasture and grain in abundance; the meadows are vast and richly watered with springs and rivulets; the trees are large and the fruits are exquisite; everywhere there are springs and rivers. Do not fear to come; no one will hinder you or drive you away.' On hearing this news, the Banū Merīn immediately set out for the West, after recommending themselves to Almighty God. From halting-place to halting-place they came on their horses and camels, with their flocks, their baggage and their tents. They arrived in such numbers that their multitude was like unto the rain or unto the stars of the night-sky . . .

They found that the Almohad kings no longer cared about their duty and were given over to wine, luxury and debauchery. So they continued uninterruptedly to enter their country and began to conquer their fortified places. For it was God's will that they should rule over the Maghrib, and like a swarm of locusts they soon covered the whole land. Energetic and courageous in battle, they continued to consolidate their power, taking possession of one district after another, until finally in 613 (1216 A.D.) they defeated the Almohad army . . . (*Rawḍ al-Qirṭās*)

The Merinids, who made Fez the capital of their empire, were in no way destructive towards city culture, but on the contrary gave encouragement to science and art. At the same time, in Andalusia, they continued the fight against the Christian kingdoms until they had exhausted all their strength. Finally they were compelled, both in Spain and in parts of central Morocco where other remnants of the Almohads had made themselves independent, to retreat step by step. Nevertheless the Andalusian Muslims, who were now returning in increasing numbers, brought to Morocco and especially to Fez a new flowering of city culture. Granada was the last refuge of Moorish culture in Spain; Fez was to be its heir.

The fall of the Merinid dynasty at the turn of the fifteenth century was followed by the weaker rule of the Wattāsids (Banū Wattās) who, as stewards of their predecessors took over power. From now on Morocco was forced on to the defensive: in the fifteenth century the Portuguese attacked the north coast of the country, and at the beginning of the sixteenth they took several strong-points on the Atlantic coast, to as far south as Agadir. With the development of navigation and military technology in modern Europe, the natural relationship of forces changed once and for all. Now the threat came not from the desert but from the sea; and the Wattāsid horsemen were unable to cope with the sea-going conquerors who set upon the country from the Atlantic ocean. Yet in response to this dire threat there awoke in the people itself, in a variety of areas more or less independent of the Sultan, the will to fight for their faith.

THE SAADIANS

From the time of the Merinids, the absence of a ruler whom all could look upon as the true representative or Caliph of the Prophet had produced a profound transformation in the mentality of the people. The individual tribes rallied more and more to spiritual leaders who, as the heads of spiritual orders or as the descendants of the Prophet, embodied the tradition of Islam. It was this general trend, which was arising everywhere, that brought to power the Saadians, whose forebears traced their descent from the family of the Prophet, and who had only recently migrated into southern Morocco. In the Sūs, where the Portuguese attack had reached its furthest point, two brothers of this family took over the leadership of the resistance, and one of them, Muḥammad ash-Shaykh, finally rose against the Wattāsids and entered Fez as Sultan in 1549.

> When Muḥammad ash-Shaykh entered New Fez for the first time, he wore (like the Nomads of the western Sahara) an over-garment of blue linen and a red head-covering . . . This was the way in which the leaders and even the nobles (*shurafā'*) from the Drā^{c} region were dressed, up to the moment of their entering Fez and having their sovereignty recognized. For, as soon as this happened, they refined their living style under the influence of a man and a woman. The man was Qāsim Zerhūnī, who had served as vizier under the Merinids; he taught them how to improve their dress and their manners. He showed them how to wear

FAR RIGHT: *The old walls of Taroudant, a traditional market town and capital of the Sūs region.*

> their clothes and wind their turbans, how to use beautifully harnessed horses and to decorate their weapons with gold and silver; how to do business with the great and how to hold council with those who, as scholars, authors, secretaries, bodyguards and officers, enjoyed this right; how and in what order these categories should take their places at an audience, what were the times of the meals, and how guests should be served their food; also, how to promulgate decrees and prohibitions; he instructed them likewise about taxation in the Maghrib, and about the administration of the tribes . . . (*Rawḍ al-Qirṭās*)

Later the Saadians, who wished to maintain their contacts with the south, chose Marrakesh as their capital.

Since the dynasty of the Saadians did not depend on the cohesion of one single dominant tribe—an indispensable condition for exercising power, according to Ibn Khaldūn—they could only rule for as long as, and to the extent that, the population saw in them the champions of the faith. They had however to deal not only with the Christians, but also with Muslim opponents, namely the westward-thrusting Turks. They sought to play the one against the others, but in so doing they lost their authority, and were finally dispossessed of power because of dissension amongst the tribes.

It was at this time that the last Spanish Muslims, the so-called Moriscos, were expelled from Spain; a certain number of them settled in Morocco, especially in the coastal cities of Rabat and Salé where they armed ships and, as corsairs, took up the fight against their enemies the Christian Spaniards. It was thus that Morocco first began to play a certain role on the high seas, where the great battles of the century were to be fought. From the European point of view, the corsair role of the Moriscos was nothing other than piracy; but in their own eyes, however lucrative it may have been, it was ennobled by its character of fighting for the faith; and this explains why, in the corsair cities, life and civilization were the very antithesis of rough barbarism.

THE ᶜALAWITES

In the second half of the seventeenth century, the Saadians were overpowered by an Arab invasion which gave the sovereignty to the ᶜAlawite dynasty, which has retained the throne of the 'Far West' (the Maghrib) to the present day. Their forefathers had likewise recently migrated from Arabia to the Tafilelt in southern Morocco. As descendants of the Prophet they quickly assumed a leading position amongst the nomadic tribes of the south and the south-west and, having gained control of the Saharan caravan routes along which came the gold of the Sudan, they soon conquered the whole of Morocco. Thereupon Fez, which throughout all the centuries had remained the spiritual centre of the country, once again became the political capital, as it always did when Arab influence was stronger than Berber, with the sole exception of a short interlude under Sultan Mulay Ismāᶜīl, the contemporary of Louis XIV,

who relied neither on Arab nor Berber but solely on his army of Sudanese slaves, and who re-built Meknes as his royal city. It was much later, under the influence of the French protectorate, that the sultanate left Fez and transferred its seat to Rabat on the Atlantic coast.

Ibn Khaldūn had demonstrated how political or royal power had its foundation in tribal cohesion or coalition and how, whenever this power lost its momentum, the (by now) city-based rulers were overwhelmed by a new wave of desert nomads. Since the seventeenth century this 'law' seems no longer to have applied. Although the ʿAlawite dynasty gradually lost the support of the Arab tribes and became too weak to subdue completely the Berbers of the Middle and High Atlas, it was never overthrown by any new wave of conquerors from the desert. The new element that disturbed the quasi-natural course of events came from modern Europe. It was the first harbinger of technological warfare in the form of a few cannons, thanks to which the fortified towns henceforth became impregnable to the Bedouins; but these cannons were nevertheless insufficient to hold permanently in check either the nomads of the vast plains or the inhabitants of the inaccessible mountain valleys. Mulay Ismāʿīl, thanks to his black army and his implacable severity, succeeded once again in subduing at least the area north of the Atlas; after him, and at the end of a long crisis, it was the intrepid Mulay Ḥasan I who maintained the political unity of the country, at the price of interminable campaigns against rebel tribes, until his death in 1894; then Morocco, already harassed by the colonial powers, gradually disintegrated into a loosely knit confederation of tribes.

> The more familiar I become with the ways of Morocco, wrote a French diplomat in 1866, the more I am impressed how similar this country is to our European society of the Middle Ages. It is ruled by more or less independent feudal lords, who are far from recognizing the sultan as their head. The sultan's authority is purely nominal in respect of two thirds of what is called his empire. The majority of the tribes—and I speak only of those in the north of the country, for the south of the Atlas things are quite different—bow to his spiritual prestige; they see in him the descendant of the Prophet and are happy to mention his name in the Friday prayer. But many of them, and naturally the most warlike amongst them, want to hear nothing about the sultan when political affairs are at stake. They do not accept the officials appointed by him, or at best accept them in name only, granting them no power to act. They pay him no taxes, but at best occasionally send him—not as a recognized obligation, but only as a pious gift to the descendant of Muḥammad—a kind of Muslim 'Peter's pence'—a sum of money, the amount of which is decided by themselves. As for the tribes who are subject to the sultan, they behave towards him

> like the vassals of the Middle Ages: they owe the lord financial and military aid, which they furnish according to the circumstances; otherwise they administer themselves as seems best to them under the leadership of their *caïds*, whose authorization in office by the sultan is little more than a formality. The sultan is absolute master only of his own domain, that is to say, in the large towns and their surroundings, rather like the King of France in the Middle Ages, who essentially was only the first and the strongest of the princes of the land . . . (*Charmes*)

This state of affairs was by no means only a disadvantage for the happiness of the people, as can be seen when one compares it with the paralysing effect of the administration, complete with officials, imposed by the Turks in the more eastern parts of the Maghrib. Morocco remained the place of refuge of an unbroken tradition and retained all its inward values. One reason for this was the fact that the towns, because of the increasing encirclement of Morocco and the resulting decrease in trade, did not fall victim to the moral laxity into which Oriental cities, more rapidly than European ones, tend to slip, once they are abandoned to themselves. At any rate, the spiritual principles on which the traditional culture of the Islamic west was founded remained for the time being intact. In the Orient—and the Islamic 'west' is spiritually part of the Orient—there are no secular or atheistic revolutions except those implanted from Europe. Materialism, which inevitably enjoys an upsurge whenever there is spiritual arrest, receives no philosophical expression from purely Oriental sources; it remains but a matter of sensual enjoyments.

During the years 1830 to 1848 the French conquered Algeria. The Emir ᶜAbd al-Qādir took up the struggle against them, and attempted to win over Morocco to his cause. He possessed all the spiritual and political qualities that a renewer of the western caliphate ought to have, but precisely this was one of the reasons why the Moroccan sultan Mulay ᶜAbd ar-Raḥmān, under pressure from the French, left him in the lurch. In so doing Morocco bought peace with France, for a few short years.

THE ARRIVAL OF THE FRENCH

In 1907 the French, on the pretext of protecting their trading settlements, established themselves on the Atlantic coast. Their presence upset the shaky equilibrium of the tribes. Sultan Mulay Ḥafīẓ's failure to stop the French advance increased the discontent of certain tribes in the north and provoked a rising against him which had been threatening for some time. The sultan felt compelled to accept the aid, half offered and half imposed, of the French army, and finally, in 1912, to accept the French protectorate over his whole kingdom.

The French undertook to make the rebelling tribes submit to the Sultan. For France, this was an opportunity to lay its hands, politically and economically, on Morocco. The commitment that France accepted towards the ruling house was in entire conformity with what it deemed to be its true mission, namely 'civilization', which, for Europeans in general and the French in particular, means the promotion of sedentarism and urbanization, and the gradual elimination of nomadism. The French conquerors and colonizers saw themselves as successors to the Romans, and even the romantic enthusiasm which some of them felt at the encounter with the authentic Moroccan way of life was nourished by the image of Rome: 'Rome is no longer Rome', exclaimed the painter Delacroix; 'the ancient world has nothing more beautiful to offer than these sons of the desert in their robes!'

In the eyes of the European conquerors, the whole history of Morocco up to the establishment of the French protectorate was characterized by the constantly repeated failure of nation-forming forces:

> Morocco has never found a solution for the political and social questions to which the great powers in the west found an answer by founding, firstly, enduring dynastic states, and soon thereafter, nations.
>
> It even seems that Morocco, like all Barbary, never sought to formulate such a solution . . . The great historian and sociologist of Muslim Barbary, Ibn Khaldūn, could only conceive of a kind of historical determinism without issue and without hope. After brilliantly analysing the past and present history of his country, lucidly portraying the intimate life of the Berber tribes and the actions of the dynasties, and describing in a gripping way the destructive work of the Arab Bedouins, he neither sees nor seeks any remedy to this rhythmical recurrence of catastrophes. This diabolic cycle of failures and miseries appears to him as an inevitable law of history. The thought of progress, or of an ideal, never seems even to have crossed the mind of this man who, in western Islam, was the leading light of his time and the greatest authority on the political and social realities of Barbary. (*Terrasse*)

This criticism completely overlooks the fact that the idea of progress in a straight line, that has dominated European history for the last few centuries, is nothing other than the latter-day secularization of the Christian expectation of the Kingdom of God, and therefore could never arise in the mind of a medieval Muslim author. Ibn Khaldūn saw things in the light of a spiritual realism that clearly distinguishes between the fate of an individual and that of a collectivity; only the individual has it in him fully to realize a spiritual prototype, because inwardly he is free; on the other hand, a collectivity—like every multiplicity—can never escape certain constraints; the best that can happen is a more or less long-lasting balance of forces, within which the individual can follow his own goal: the salvation of his soul. To strive after a perfect happiness for all on the earthly plane, as if it were possible to establish peace and well-being permanently, can only lead to the gravest deception, and consequently to damage to the soul, for the individual as for the collectivity.

Like the Christian culture of the Middle Ages, Islamic culture is shaped by its spiritual origin, while modern civilization on the contrary looks towards the future. Since the origin is of God, and since everything that comes thereafter can at best be only a reflection of this, the world, taken over all, can never become better. As the Prophet Muḥammad expressed it: 'Every century after this one will be worse than its predecessor.' The believing Muslim knows this, and this also explains why Muslim culture in its later phases is much less dynamic than the rationalistic culture of Europe, in which the spiritual highpoint of life is not the contemplation of the eternal verities and their realization in the soul, but scientific and technological adventure. When the Europeans introduced electric lighting into newly occupied Tangier, a shaykh remarked: 'If these people were obliged to pray five times a day, they would have no time for such childishness!' There is more in this observation than may immediately meet the eye.

Like every revealed and traditional culture Islam sees in the future, not man but God. The future is attained only by whatever has its roots in the Divine past. The history of Morocco is nothing other than a constantly recurring will to re-establish the Origin with a view to the Divine End; for God is 'the Inheritor', (*al-Wārith*), unto Whom all things return and before Whose throne all men will be assembled on Doomsday: *Verily we are God's*, says the Koran, *and verily unto Him do we return.*

ITO'S CAVE

I was once a guest in the cave village of the Aït Tserrūsh ('the sons of the jackal'), a Berber tribe of the Middle Atlas. When I woke up in the morning, I did not at first understand why I was surrounded by uneven patches of semi-darkness. But when I turned over on my sheepskin I saw, through the narrow cave mouth, the brilliant light of day. A soft whimpering had awakened me: in one of the large niches that opened out from all around the inside wall of the cave, there lay a small Berber child who was wriggling under some earth-coloured blankets. All of a sudden, in the section of sky cut out by the cave mouth, I could see Ito, the child's mother, who had appeared in response to his cry. She put down a jug of water, picked up the child, and laid him on her lap in order to suckle him. Once more in the cave all was silent; one could barely hear, in the distance, the sounds of the day: the cry of an animal or the clattering of hooves. The Berber woman sat in the half-light, motionless as a rock.

When the infant was satisfied, she let it slide to the ground, sat down in front of a mortar, and began to grind wheat. She sieved the flour, mixed it with water in a wooden bowl, and then kneaded the dough with powerful and regular movements. Finally she divided the dough into six equal-sized balls, which she carefully flattened into circular pieces of bread, having first kept behind in the bowl a piece of dough about the size of an apple, which would be used to leaven the next day's batch.

Ito was too powerful and too solid to be truly beautiful. But her broad face,

Berber mother and child.

with its wide-open eyes, looked as if it had been carved out of some bright stone, and shone with a proud and powerful femininity. She carried her dignity with an innocent awareness. Tattoo marks on her forehead and chin both decorated and protected her.

The air in the cave smelled slightly of stone. At this depth one is protected both from the heat of the day and the cold of the night. The world above seemed no longer to be of any concern, and the cave enveloped one maternally; one felt a reluctance to climb up to the hot ground above, rather as if one struggled not to be born.

Once more someone filled the small piece of sky. The child's father, Mohaudris, made his way down. He was a young Berber with regular features and an impenetrable expression, as if he bore on his countenance the reflection of the vast and rocky steppe. He was dressed in a wide, white shirt, and had a narrow turban round his head. Over his shoulders hung a *'selham'* or burnous (a simple cloak of rough wool), on the back of which a long cross was embroidered—perhaps the sign of the remote Christian origin of his tribe. His name, Mohaudris, is the Berber abbreviation of the double name Muḥammad Idrīs.

'Peace be upon thee', came his greeting, 'blessed be the morning, may no harm befall thee!' He had brought with him the head of a young goat, and set about preparing it for my breakfast.

I asked him about the life of the community in which I was a guest. A part of the population had gone into the mountains with their tents to pasture their sheep and goats. Those remaining behind attended to the fields of maize which lay further down in the valley.

My horse was tethered in a neighbouring cave. When I led him a few yards up into the daylight, he shied at first, as if blinded by the sun. On the surface of the ground, all one could see of the village were the cave openings protected by thorn bushes and a defensive wall that surrounded everything. Looking towards the north, over the edge of the plateau, one could just make out the large yellow hollow in which Fez lay. To the south extended the undulating steppe, a vast plateau where, in the spring, exquisite flowers appear amongst the boulders; but now, in summer, the bare ground was decorated only by tough bushes such as broom and juniper.

On a hill nearby a new mosque had been built. This was the tribes' answer to a French edict promising the Berbers their own legislation independent of that of the Koran. 'Why does the Rumi (the European) covet my stony valley?' asks a Berber song, 'he who possesses everything that a man can desire? Does he reach out his hand to snatch the faith from my heart?'

The mosque was built of gigantic cedar trunks from the mountains in the south. The outside walls and the flat roof were covered with sun-dried mud. In the inside, trunks with their bark removed stood in rows like high, reddish pillars. The archaic impression made by this building, in its powerful simplicity, was increased even further by the earnest faces of the Berbers, who stood or sat between the cedar pillars. In the faces of several of the older men there was a profound concentration and resignation.

From one end of the village could be heard the haunting sounds of a flute, accompanied by a dull, steady drumbeat. It was the music of a Sufi brotherhood that was rooted amongst the people of the region. The musicians were standing in front of a cave entrance and a Berber woman gyrated in an ecstatic dance. Her hair, held together by a woven ribbon, became undone because of her rapid movements, and swirled through the air like a large black bird.

In the centre of the village, beautiful children were playing. And heavily laden beasts of burden entered the village through the gate.

On the horizon of the great plain, down to which I was now riding, there were still some fine strips of morning cloud, light pink in colour. The light of dawn sparkled on the dark metallic-looking leaves of the dwarf palms which covered the slopes. Gradually the brown earth flattened out, and seemed to stretch endlessly ahead of me. The caravan track was covered with a network of cracks, and left and right stood desiccated thistles, which looked as if they were made out of blue glass. Further away were low black tents, and half-wild dogs barked at me as I passed.

The Moroccan earth, which from June onwards is almost bare, is everywhere near to man. The Bedouin sleeps on it and rests on it, and his cloak, however often he may wash it, always has in it something of the earth on which he lives. Nothing separates man from the immense and austere body of the earth, which nowhere has an end. But the sunlight filling the sky, the sunlight unobscured by any mist, relieves the earth of its heaviness and unites all things, without suppressing their proper forms, in its infinite crystal.

Towards midday I reached the first wheatfields, already mown, and then the villages of the *fellāḥīn* whose white houses of sun-dried mud rested like sarcophagi on the vast plain. A stallion tethered in front of one of the houses raised its head, and neighed loudly. While the flocks crouched down together on top of their own shadows—the sun being now almost vertically above them—I rested awhile beside a well, under an acacia tree. Then I rode on in the direction of Fez, and the nearer I came to the city, the more I overtook small caravans of mules and donkeys making their way there with loads of cedar logs, animal skins or goatskin bottles full of olive oil. Many had come from afar, having trotted for days over the rocky plateau.

The sun was already sinking before I could see, in the distance, the hills surrounding Fez, with their bright, ochre-coloured ridges and silvery green clumps of olive trees. No sooner had the sun set than the scene was transformed into a world of antique gold, jade and opal, beneath a sky of turquoise.

Slowly the colours were extinguished like a dying brazier. The earth retreated and the sky opened up, a measureless ocean with silvery islands and shimmering shores. Underneath, the caravans, as if drunk with sleep, followed their drovers' song.

3 The Caliphate

A THEOCRATIC STATE

THE PROTOTYPICAL Islamic state is theocratic, for in it spiritual power and temporal power are combined. Herein it differs from the traditional Christian state which, in view of Christ's words 'My kingdom is not of this world', can never be identified with the Church. From the Christian point of view spiritual authority, which must always prefer the law of God to that of the world, is not compatible with temporal power, which in order to exist, has to take account of political—therefore natural and this-worldly—pressures arising from within the community.

From the Islamic point of view, however, things present themselves differently: the Prophet was both 'Messenger of God' and temporal ruler; the Koran is both a spiritual teaching and a legislation; it contains not only a moral law that applies to the individual, but also a social law that applies to the community. Islam means 'submission' to the Will of God, and this has been revealed on earth as a determined order valid for one and all. This order takes full account of the natural needs of the collectivity, and, from this point of view, to show respect for political forces, such as military and royal power, is above all a question of equilibrium, which itself represents an aspect of Islam.

Consequently the caliph who, as representative (*khalīfa*) of the Prophet, exercises the highest office in the Islamic community, is not really comparable to the highest priest in the Christian sense of the word; he is above all the highest judge, so that his authority may be compared not so much to that of pope or patriarch, as to that of the emperor of the Holy Roman Empire in the Middle Ages. He is indeed the officiant (*imām*) at the communal prayers and also, when necessary, the highest judge in matters of faith, but he is not the minister of any sacraments, since in Islam there is no consecrated priesthood.

Thus the caliph embodies both the office of the *imām*, who presides over the communal prayers and is responsible for the correct performance of divine worship, and the office of supreme judge; he is commander-in-chief of the forces for the defence of the community, whence his title *Emir al-mu'minīn* (Commander of the Faithful), and in cases where the doctors of the law fail to reach agreement, he has the right of final judgement. According to Ibn Khaldūn he has the power to invest others with authority in regard to policing, public prosecution, commercial administration, and the public mint.

Ibn Khaldūn describes the meaning of the caliphate as follows:

> Kingship or royalty is the expression of an irreplaceable order in human society. It requires sovereignty and power, which depend on the aggressive and therefore animal nature of man. This is why it may degenerate into despotism. The despot makes demands which exceed the capacity of his subjects. The situation may vary according to the attitude of different generations, but it always leads to the point where obedience becomes intolerable, so that unrest and the shedding of blood occur. It is therefore mandatory that the ruler should observe certain laws recognized by the people themselves . . .
>
> If these laws are formulated by enlightened members of the royal house, they create a political order founded on reason. But if they are ordained by God Himself, as laws of faith, the result is a political order founded on faith, and this is useful both for the present life, and for the life to come.
>
> For the purpose of earthly life is not merely earthly well-being. The whole world is perishable and vain; its end is death and destruction. God has said: *Think ye then that We have created you for nothing?* (Koran 23:115) The meaning of human life lies in religion, which leads to bliss in the next world; religion is the way of God, to whom *all that is in Heaven and on earth belong* (Koran 42:53) . . . This also applies to royalty, which results from the natural structure of human society . . . Any overlordship that depends merely on brute force or the arbitrary play of natural aggressiveness becomes tyranny or injustice and contradicts the laws of religion as well as flying in the face of political wisdom. But, at the same time, whatever results exclusively from mere political considerations and intentions, without being governed by religious laws, is worthless, since it springs from a view of things that is deprived of divine light: *Whom God doth not illumine, he hath no light.* (Koran 24:40) . . .
>
> This explains the meaning of the caliphate: natural kingship commands the people by instinct and desire; politically-inspired leadership causes it to act in respect of a rational appreciation of earthly advantages and disadvantages; but the caliphate guides the people with a view to its well-being both in this world and in the next . . . Thus in fact the caliphate represents the Lawgiver (Muḥammad), since like him it must protect religion as well as exercising political sovereignty in this world . . . (*Muqaddima* 3:23)

From all of this it results that kingship, as the natural foundation of the caliphate, belongs to the Islamic form of state.

The question of the legitimacy of the caliphate split the Muslim world in two. The Shiites, to which group the majority of Persians belong, take the view that only a physical descendant of ᶜAlī, the nephew and son-in-law of the Prophet, may be proclaimed Caliph; they consequently reject not only the first three Caliphs, Abū Bakr, Omar and Othman, but also all Caliphs subsequent to the fourth Caliph, ᶜAlī. They believe that, in every age, a hidden *imām* from the posterity of ᶜAlī possesses the true succession to the Prophet. The Sunnis, on the other hand—and this includes the people of the Maghrib— require only that a caliph should possess the spiritual and moral qualities that his function demands, as well as the might necessary to make this respected. In general they believe that the caliph should be a descendant of the paternal tribe of the

A festive crowd awaits the arrival of the Sultan.

Prophet, the Quraysh; but Ibn Khaldūn considers that this condition does not apply since the time when the Quraysh lost their hegemony in the Arab world. The caliphate, according to him, must of necessity have a real power base; as an institution for this world, it cannot be bound to an ideal without reality 'for the law of religion cannot rightly demand something that is in contradiction to the law of nature . . .' (*Muqaddima* 3:24) It would be impossible to express more clearly the contrast between the Muslim and the Christian ethos.

The origin and prototype of the Moroccan state is the caliphate—or imāmate—which was founded by Idrīs ibn ᶜAbdallāh al-Kāmil towards the end of the eighth century. Idrīs was the grandson of Ḥasan, one of the two sons of ᶜAlī, the fourth Caliph, and Fāṭima, the daughter of the Prophet. Fleeing from the Abbasid caliph, who had put him to flight as a potential rival, he reached the Far West in 172 A.H. (788 A.D.) and found refuge in the erstwhile Roman city of Volubilis (Ulili) on Mount Zerhūn, which was inhabited by the Berber Awrabā tribe. Our Lord Idrīs, writes al-Kattānī,

> was the first man of the family of the Prophet known to have reached the Maghrib . . . At that time Isḥāq ibn ᶜAbdallāh, a muᶜtazilite, was prince of the Awrabā. He received Mulay Idrīs warmly, and persuaded the surrounding Berber tribes to enter into alliance with him . . .
>
> (*Salwāt al-Anfās*)

This meant that they recognized Idrīs as the legitimate pretender to the Caliphate and they undertook to obey him on condition that he upheld the Koranic law. This alliance, without which no caliph can assume his function and which is generally concluded by a handshake between him and the doctors of the law as the responsible leaders of the community (*al-umma*), finds its prototype in the pact which the Prophet, when he was put to flight by the Meccans, concluded with his companions-in-arms: they promised him, while taking his hand, to fight for the cause of Islam, unto victory or death. *God's hand is over their hands,* says the Koran regarding this incident, *whoso breaketh the pact, breaketh it on his own responsibility; but whoso fulfilleth what he hath promised to God, will receive from Him an immense reward.*

By thus turning away from the Abbasids, and choosing a descendant of ᶜAlī and Fāṭima as Imām, the Berber tribes of the Gharb adopted an attitude similar to that of the Shiites in the great dispute over the caliphate. Soon afterwards, under the influence of the Umayyad caliphate in Córdoba, they opted for the Mālikite-Sunni system of law, but the example of the Idrīsids continued to have its effects; loyalty to the family of the Prophet runs through the history of Morocco like a scarlet thread; Ibn Tūmart relied on his descent from the Prophet, and, when defence against the Christian conquerors was required, the Saadian and ᶜAlawite dynasties, both *shurafā'*, were called to the throne. *Shurafā'* (in the singular: *sharīf*) means 'noble', and is used to designate descendants of the Prophet.

The first wave of Muslim conquerors who, within seventy years of the Prophet's death, had reached the Straits of Gibraltar and who immediately thereafter swarmed across Spain and into France, taking with them an army of Berbers, had affected western Barbary only superficially, and had nowhere left behind them a permanent spiritual centre around which all the existing tendencies towards Islam could crystallize. A large section of the Berbers adhered to Judaism, others were Monophysite Christians, and the majority were pagans or members of strange sects comprising a diversity of elements. Only the appearance of a man such as Idrīs, who combined the hallowed nobility of his descent with the qualities of a spiritual and political leader, could create the centre around which a homogeneous Islamic culture might begin to form. During his five-year reign Idrīs I extended his theocratic kingdom over almost the whole of Northern Morocco. When, in 792 or 793, he was poisoned by a secret emissary of the Abbasid caliph, his son Idrīs II was not yet born. The latter was destined to extend his father's empire even further, and to found the city of Fez.

The Arab chroniclers attribute to both Idrīs I and Idrīs II all the natural and spiritual virtues that should adorn a true descendant of the Prophet.

> In everything he did, writes al-Kattānī of Idrīs II, he always held fast to the Truth. His judgements were always in accord with sacred law. He never deviated from the law or custom of the Prophet. Thus each year he received a tithe, without making the slightest change in the prescribed measure, and distributed this to whom it was due, namely the weak, the poor, and the orphans. When booty was brought to him following a military expedition, he returned four-fifths to the combatants, and retained only one-fifth for his own purposes . . . (*Salwāt al-Anfās*)

It was not without reason that legend likened his justice to the practice of the Prophet regarding the distribution of tithes and booty, for in this field lay the greatest temptation for a ruler.

In Morocco Mulay Idrīs I is called Mulay Idrīs al-Akbar: 'Our Lord Idrīs the Elder'. Mulay, Our Lord, is the title given there to all descendants of the Prophet. The Moroccans regard his tomb as their greatest sanctuary. The mosque containing his tomb is in the middle of a small white town which lies on a rocky spur of Mount Zerhūn, a little above the hill on which are ruins of the ancient city of Volubilis. The shepherds in this area call the ruins 'Pharaoh's Castle' (*Qaṣr-Firᶜūn*).

When one is travelling in a westerly direction from Fez to Meknes, one sees Mount Zerhūn arising on the horizon like a wave with three crests. On horseback, one can reach it in one night and half a day.

From the east side, the sanctuary cannot be seen. All around the diadem of

The holy town of Mulay Idrīs on Mount Zerhūn.

the mount one can see only little villages and solitary domes, shining like clear pearls in a celestially blue light. But on the west side, the crown of the summit lies open, and from below one can recognize the white triangle of the little town against a dark background of age-old olive trees. Like holy mountains all over the world, Mount Zerhūn stands free on all sides, and towers over the surrounding country.

In this small holy town, which is called Mulay Idrīs, no unbeliever may dwell. The sepulchral mosque, surrounded by closely packed houses, consists of several buildings, rather like a far-eastern temple precinct; a covered alleyway leads into the first courtyard, onto which open the vast halls of the mosque, their ceilings supported by pillars. A further alleyway connects the first courtyard with a second; here alms are distributed daily to the poor and the sick, and on one side of this courtyard is a Koran school. Finally, through yet another doorway, one reaches the innermost courtyard, surrounded by rows of pillars, in the middle of which a large fountain plays. Only from here can one gain access to the high, square hall, surmounted by a honeycomb dome of cedarwood, which houses the tomb of the holy prince. The position of this is marked by a filigree shrine, draped in a silken covering. Here such a deep silence reigns, that even the splashing of the fountain is lost in it. Men sit motionless on the carpets surrounding the tomb, and their rosaries glide through their fingers. Women enshrouded in white kneel at the threshold of

Berber horsemen riding at the festival of Mulay Idrīs.

the tomb and whisper prayers. Only tiny children run about on silent feet and creep under the silken covering of the shrine in order to get even closer to the saint with their petitions. Here the heart of Morocco beats in silence.

Once a year a festival springs into life around the sanctuary. When this happens, crowds of pilgrims from all parts of the country turn the olive groves surrounding the town into an enormous camp of tents of all kinds. Representatives from all the tribes, accompanied by their mounted entourage and by musicians offer sacrificial animals. Equestrian competitions are held in honour of the saint, and members of Sufi brotherhoods sing to the beating of drums.

That the caliphate can never again attain the perfection that it possessed at its origin is accepted by Moroccans—as by all Muslims—as an inevitable consequence of the declining times. They also know that a reciprocal relationship exits between people and king.

'The corruption of the people', said the Maghribi saint Abū Madyan, 'gives rise to tyrants, and the corruption of the great gives rise to revolts and heresies.'

Originally it was generally believed that the whole Islamic world should come under one caliph; but because of the wide geographical distribution of the Muslim peoples, it was finally accepted as inevitable that several caliphs should rule at the same time. The less able the Maghribi caliphate was to lay claim to the whole of the Islamic world, the greater the importance its subjects laid on the *sharīfian* descent of their caliph. For the Moroccans, their ruler is *imām* first and foremost because he is descended from the Prophet. Thus Morocco enjoys the title of '*Sharīfian* Kingdom', in reference to the ruling dynasty, whose theocratic character represents the last bulwark against the secularization of the Moroccan state.

The expectation that at some future time the perfect caliphate will be miraculously re-established, is founded on a saying of the Prophet, according to which, towards the end of the age, a man of his posterity will rally the Islamic community and restore the law in all its purity. This is the 'Rightly-guided one', the *Mahdī*, whom the Almohads had considered to be Ibn Tūmart.

If, in view of its temporal basis, the Maghribi caliphate possessed much more power than did a Christian patriarch or pope, it was nevertheless at the same time much more restricted as to the worldly measures it could take, than was any European principality. This explains why the Moroccan rulers, who towards the end of the nineteenth century were urged by the European nations, with polite threats, to open up their country to modern trade and industry, were in such a difficult position. Their outward power was undermined to the extent that it showed itself to be inadequate in the face of the technical development of Europe that had come with the age of rationalism, whereas its claim to power with regard to its own subjects lay precisely in its being able to maintain, in as pure a state as possible, the Islamic form of life, with its almost monastic austerity and frugality, its contempt for all haste, and its high esteem for the traditional sciences whose foundation lay in the Koran.

Pierre Loti, who as part of a French embassy paid a visit to Sultan Mulay al-Ḥasan in 1889, was to a certain extent able to sense this contradictory and basically tragic situation of the sovereign, without however fully understanding it. In the diary of his journey, he wrote, under the date of 27 April, as follows:

> This morning we were introduced to the Sultan . . . At half past eight we all assembled in formal dress in the Moorish courtyard of the house occupied by our minister and his entourage.
>
> Then the 'introducer of ambassadors' arrived, a gigantic mulatto with the neck of a bull, who carried an enormous stick. (The largest man in the kingdom is always chosen for this office.) Four men in long white robes appeared with him, and remained motionless behind him, all carrying sticks similar to his, in the manner of a drum major, with arms outstretched. These people were there simply to hold back the crowd.
>
> When it was time for us to mount our horses, we crossed the garden of orange trees, while the mild winter rain that had accompanied us for the whole of our journey, continued to fall. We made our way to the lower gate that opens onto the street. Here our horses were brought to us one by one, as the street was too narrow for them either to turn round or to come

forward two abreast. We mounted at random whichever horses were nearest, in haste, and without any order . . .

As on the day of our arrival, we crossed the empty spaces that divide Old Fez from New Fez, and proceeded to pass by large rocks, aloe trees, caves, tombs, ruins, and heaps of decaying animal bodies, above which birds were circling.

Finally we reached the first enclosure of the palace and, through a large gateway with a horseshoe arch, we entered the courtyard of the ambassadors.

This courtyard was so vast, that I know of no city in the world that has one to compare with it. It was surrounded by enormous crenellated walls, flanked by heavy bastions—like the ramparts of Istanbul, Damietta or Aigues-Mortes—but rather more dilapidated, more menacing and more sinister. Wild grass was growing there and, in the middle, there was a pond where frogs were croaking. The sky was dark and in movement: showers of birds rose from the crenellated towers and whirled round above us.

The place seemed empty, in spite of the thousands of men ranged against the four walls: the same people as always, and the same colours; on the one side a white multitude in burnous and hood; on the other side a red multitude, the troops of the sultan, accompanied by their musicians, in long orange, green, violet, yellow or gold robes. The central part of the vast courtyard, towards which we now advanced, remained completely empty. And at such a distance all the people tightly packed against the huge, crenellated walls seemed like Lilliputians.

Through a bastion at one of its corners, this courtyard is linked with the precincts of the palace . . .

The troops began to move: red soldiers and brightly clad musicians formed two long rows, creating a kind of avenue that extended from the centre of the courtyard where we stood to the bastion through which the sultan was to appear. We all looked towards the arabesque-adorned doorway and awaited his most holy majesty.

This doorway was more than two hundred yards away from us, so immense was the courtyard, and through it came first of all several great dignitaries, viziers with long white beards and dark faces; today all were on foot, as we ourselves now were, and they walked slowly within the floating white of their veils and burnouses. We already knew almost all of these personalities, whom we had seen on our arrival the day before yesterday, but then in prouder procession, mounted on their beautiful horses. Also came the *caïd* Belail, the black court jester, his head as always surmounted by his impossibly high and dome-shaped turban. He moved forward on his own, in a grotesque rolling gait, supporting himself on an enormous cudgel; there was something disquieting and mocking in his whole person, which seemed to be fully confident that he enjoyed the highest favour.

The sky remained menacing; storm clouds propelled by a strong wind ran races in the heavens with flocks of birds, and only here and there could we see small areas of blue sky, which reminded us that we were in the country of clear light. The walls and towers bristled everywhere with their sharp crenellations and looked like gigantic combs with their teeth pointing upwards. They entirely surrounded us, as if within a vast and fantastic citadel. Time had bestowed on them a rare golden greyish colour. They were full of crevices, indented and loose, and looked as old as the hills. Two or three storks blinked down from them on the crowd below, and a mule with a red-upholstered saddle which—I know not how—had clambered onto one of the towers, looked down also. Our attention was more and more concentrated on the arabesque-decorated door, through which there now came about fifty little black slaves, dressed in red, and draped in white muslin cloaks, and looking like choir-boys. They walked forward gravely, huddling closely together like a flock of sheep.

These were followed by six magnificent white horses, all saddled and harnessed in silk, and rearing frequently as they were led forward.

Then came a few more minutes of waiting and silence; suddenly a tremor of pious awe ran through the hedge of soldiers. The music, with its large trumpets and drums, resounded loudly and eerily. The fifty little black slaves began to run, and spread out like a fan, or like swarming birds or bees. In the distance, in the shadow of the horse-shoe arch on which our attention remained fixed, a tall white mummy-like figure with a brown countenance, enshrouded in muslin, had appeared on a superb white horse led by four slaves. Above his head they supported a red parasol of ancient design, such as the parasol of the Queen of Sheba must have been like; and two tall Negroes, one in pink and one in blue, waved fly-chasers in front of his face.

As the strange horseman advanced towards us, almost formless, but deeply impressive under the mass of his white garments, the plaintive music rang out in even louder and shriller tones, accompanied by fearsome drumbeats. The horse of the mummy-like figure capered wildly, and was held in check only with difficulty by the black slaves. And our nervous systems continued to be assailed by the eerie and unfamiliar music.

Finally he was there, directly in front of us, this last authentic son of Muḥammad, of half-Nubian blood. His dress, a cloud of muslin of fine wool, was of immaculate whiteness. His horse was likewise completely white; his stirrups were of gold; his saddle and harness of silk were pale green and embroidered in light greenish-gold. The slaves who led the horse, the one who held the large red parasol and the two—dressed respectively in pink and blue—who waved white kerchiefs to chase away imaginary flies from the sovereign's person, were herculean Negroes with awesome smiles. They were all elderly, and their grey or white beards contrasted with their black faces. And all this ceremonial from another age harmonized perfectly with the wailing music and with the gigantic walls of the courtyard . . .

The man who thus ceremonially approached us was the last true representative of a religion and a culture that are destined to disappear. He was the very personification of ancient Islam. For it is known that strict Muslims consider the Sultan of Istanbul to be a usurper, and turn their thoughts and prayers towards the Maghrib where, in their view, the true successor to the Prophet resides.

What is the point of an embassy to such a sovereign who, like his people, dwells in age-old dreams that have almost vanished from the face of the earth? We are completely incapable of understanding one another. The distance between us is rather like the distance that would separate us from a caliph of Córdoba or of Baghdad, should he after a thousand years, return to earth. What do we want of him, and why have we caused him to emerge from his impenetrable palace?

His brown parchment-like face, surrounded by white veils, has regular and noble features, and lifeless eyes, whose whites can be seen under pupils that are half covered by his eyelids. His expression is one of great melancholy, lassitude, and weariness. He has an air of gentleness, and he is indeed gentle, according to those who approach him. (According to the people of Fez, he is far too mild, and does not cause enough heads to roll!) But his mildness is no doubt relative and, like that of a medieval sovereign, would not scruple at shedding blood, when this might be necessary, or at ordering a garland of severed heads to be placed on the horse-shoe arches at the entrance to a palace. But he is not cruel. With this gently sad expression, he could not be so. As his divine right so entitles him, he sometimes punishes severely, but it is said that he greatly prefers to show mercy. He is priest and warrior, and he is both to the ultimate degree. Imbued, like a prophet, with his mission from heaven, chaste in the middle of his seraglio, faithful to the most exacting religious observances, and fanatical by heredity, he seeks to imitate Muḥammad as faithfully as is humanly possible. One can moreover read all this in his eyes, in his beautiful face, and in his majestically correct attitude. He is someone who, in our day and age, we are no longer capable of understanding or of judging. But he is assuredly someone great and venerable...

And now, for a moment, he stood before us creatures from another world, with a faint astonishment and even timidity, that lent to his person a singular and unexpected charm. (*Pierre Loti*)

4 A City founded by a Saint

THE FOUNDATION OF FEZ

Idrīs II, the Arab chroniclers write,

> sketched the groundplan of the city of Fez on a Thursday morning at the beginning of the month of Rabīʿ al-awwāl of the year of the Hijra 192 (808 A.D.). When he was about to begin construction, he lifted up his hands and prayed for it and its inhabitants in the following words: 'Almighty God, make of it a house of knowledge and of legal science, so that in it Thy Book may always be read and Thy laws always observed. Let its inhabitants hold fast to the Book and the Sunna, as long as Thou shalt preserve it.' And so this city never ceased to be a centre of science and of law . . . Many and varied are the benefits, blessings and graces which Fez received thanks to the prayer which its founder offered on its behalf, thus echoing the Prophet's intercession for Medina and our lord Abraham's intercession for Mecca . . .

According to an ancient Arabian tradition, which the Koran repeats, the Kaaba in Mecca was built by Abraham and his son Ishmael, at the very spot where Hagar, wandering in the desert with her infant son, found a spring by divine inspiration. Abraham's prayer for the inhabitants of the holy city of Mecca is mentioned in the Koran. In the eyes of its inhabitants, Fez, through its foundation, is something of a holy city, and a reflection of the first two cities of Islam, mentioned in the revelation. 'Apart from Fez,' writes al-Kattānī, 'I know of no other Islamic city that is so ancient and so filled with religion and science, that was founded by a true descendant of the family of the Prophet; and the resulting blessing from this has never failed . . .' (*Salwāt al-Anfās*)

More recent researches have shown that at the time of Idrīs II, Fez consisted not simply of one town, but of two. One of them, Fez as such, seems to have taken shape, on the right bank of the river, already under the reign of Idrīs I. The second, known as al-ᶜAliya, was built by Idrīs II on the left bank in the very area where his tomb now stands. This doubling of the city indicates clearly that Idrīs II had chosen it as his capital, thus conferring importance on it for the first time. According to ancient oriental custom, a conqueror never installed himself in the residential or commercial section of a city, but built his residence—which might also be looked upon as a military encampment—outside the city.

The new and flourishing royal city attracted many Arabs from Kairuan, which at that time was the largest Muslim city in the Maghrib; and, already some time before, eight hundred families had fled from Córdoba, following an

Tents outside the town of Mulay Idrīs during the annual festival in honour of its founder.

insurrection there, and settled on the other side of the river. And thus to this very day the two halves of the city, which were only amalgamated under the Almoravid Yūsuf ben Tashfīn, are still referred to as the 'Kairuanese' district (situated around the 'Kairuanese' university—*al-Qarawiyyīn*) and the 'Andalusian' district (situated around the Andalusian mosque—*al-Andalūs*). Kairuan and Córdoba were the two poles of Arab culture in the West.

By transferring his royal residence from the Zerhūn mountains to the plain of the Gharb, Idrīs II removed himself from the whims of the Berbers, and opened the door to Arab influence. All currents flowing from east to west, to the Atlantic coast and Spain—or from there back to the east—had to pass through Fez.

In contrast with all of the many medieval cities that were built on a hill, Fez, relinquishing all thought of defence, lies in a valley, in the very depth of which is situated its sanctuary, the sepulchral mosque of Mulay Idrīs. This location finds its justification in the numerous springs that gush forth in this valley,

Crowds gathered in the town square of Mulay Idrīs on the occasion of the festival.

hollowed out like an amphitheatre on a ridge separating two levels of plain. And, because of this, it was possible to divert to the city a river that flowed from the upper plain.

> It is called the river of pearls and arises in the plain to the west of the city, about six miles away, from about sixty separate springs. Its pure waters, which glide over bright gravel, are wonderful to behold. Its movement is scarcely visible until the point where it enters the town. Here it breaks into a sheaf of rivulets which flow to the various districts, feeding the fountains of the mosques, streets, and individual houses, driving mills, filling baths, irrigating gardens, and removing, on leaving the city, all refuse and impurities . . . (*Zahrat al-Ās*)

And thus Fez possesses in abundance the most precious commodity of these regions: water gives to the city its riches and its health, and decorates it in the garland of its numerous gardens, so that an unknown Arab poet has written of it:

> The dove gave the town its ring,
> The peacock gave it its royal fan,
> Its rivers are of purest wine,
> And the courtyard of each house is a wine-glass. (*Zahrat al-Ās*)

A PICTURE OF THE CITY

With its walls crowned with towers, the large sanctuary in its midst, and the various districts and streets in the central area allotted to individual crafts, Fez resembles the medieval cities of Europe. At the same time, however, it has, like almost every other Islamic urban settlement, certain entirely distinctive characteristics: whereas in almost all ancient European cities the heritage of Rome appears in the form of a geometrical plan, with cardinal axes and a forum, Fez possesses no public square (where temple and courthouse, or cathedral and townhall, would be situated), nor does it have regularly laid out streets, flanked with the façades and windows of important buildings; the arterial routes that wend their way from the various gateways to the city centre are no more than mule-tracks that follow the contours of the terrain all the way to the markets that surround the great sanctuary. The fixed, 'crystalline', element is in this case not the city structure as such, but the individual domestic building which, entirely closed to the outside world and opening only on to its own inner courtyard where it creates a world of its own, refuses to participate in the life of the street.

In the middle of the city, around the great mosques, lie the bazaars (*aswāq*, plural of *sūq*), where the narrow alleyways are covered with bamboo sunshields and sometimes with vines, so that one moves around as if inside one single building. It is here that are located the markets for all artisanal products:

View of Fez looking over the city walls.

textiles, copper vessels and pans, as well as the markets for spices, fruits, and fowls. And nearby are narrow streets, where shoemakers, tailors, saddlers, and other craftsmen apply their skill in their little open workshops, apart from those, who, for one reason or another, have settled far from the town centre, such as the potters, whose dome-shaped kilns lie along the eastern city wall, and the tanners, who have their pits on the lower reaches of the river. Fez is famous for the production of beautifully coloured leather and all kinds of leather goods such as bags, saddles, shoes and book-bindings. The coppersmiths also have their own district, where they make chiselled trays, jugs and lamps, and here a hundred hammers incessantly ring out like bells.

The residential districts surround the city centre. One can hardly register their extent, for the lanes and alleys that lead from the arterial routes to the individual houses are no more than narrow passages, flanked by high walls, that twist and turn within the honeycomb of buildings; but they suffice, for the houses 'breathe' not via the streets, but via their inner courtyards, that open up to the skies. This type of domestic architecture not merely suits the African climate; more importantly, it is founded on the Islamic conception of the family as an inviolable sanctuary. As an enclosed cell, the Moorish house bears witness to the fact that the unity indwelling in the Islamic community is

Light filters through the bamboo shades covering a market street.

completely present in each of its individual parts. Every married believer is prayer-leader (*imām*) for his own family, and in this function he is independent of the community. Every adult Muslim, who knows the Koranic prescriptions and the custom of the Prophet—the Sunna—can be the officiant at prayer for a smaller or larger community.

THE BATHS

If the lay-out of the city shows no trace of any Greco-Roman heritage, this nevertheless crops up in other ways, especially in the construction of the public baths, which resemble the thermae of later antiquity. Like these, the baths consist of several domed rooms in which the flagstones on the floor are heated from below, so that pouring water on them provides a constant source of steam. Since, in order to conserve the warmth, the walls are provided with only small air vents, everything takes place in the subdued light of candles. In this half light, clad only in loincloths, appear the naked bodies of the bathers, as well as of the bath attendants, who carry in tubs of water, and who expertly massage their customers. These baths, which are open to women during the day and to men at night, play an important role in everyday life. They are frequented not only in order to prevent disease, but also and above all, in order to conform to the Islamic requirement for cleanliness.

THE KAISSARIYA

Also pertaining to later Antiquity, and 'imperial' by its very name, the Kaissariya is that particular area reserved for trade in expensive goods, such as

Poppy-red hides on a hillside beyond the City walls.

materials, garments, jewelry, dresses, and Moroccan shoes. At night the doorways of this area are locked. In days gone by every larger Islamic town had a *kaissariya* of this sort. That of Fez lies between the sepulchral mosque of Mulay Idrīs and the university of the Kairuanese (Al-Qarawiyyīn). As regards its style, this district has nothing Greco-Roman about it; far more does it resemble Asia—Samarkand or Peshawar—or even Mongolia. Markets of this kind were once to be found all over the East, and they even reached Europe, as the Ponte Vecchio at Florence still bears witness. The light filters through the bamboo sun-shields to the street below and here and there picks out a face or a gesture from the twilight. All noise is extinguished in the recesses of the wooden shop-stalls. Only the lively tinkling of a bell penetrates all barriers: this announces the approach of the water-carrier who pours out his welcome refreshment from a black goatskin bottle.

THE INNS

Also of Greek origin is the term *funduq*—from *pandokeion*—which is applied to the inns, which also do duty as caravanserais. If one enters their courtyards, one is—although still in the town—immediately in the presence of the people and sounds of the villages and Bedouin camps and, depending on the wares unloaded, the courtyard concerned is filled with the perfume either of fruits or grains, or of tanned skins or potter's clay.

Whoever spends the night there, lying on a piece of matting in a small

whitewashed room upstairs, can hear, on the ground-floor beneath him, the stirring of animals and, in the morning, before the cock crows, before the donkey raises its raucous voice, before the cold breath of night ceases, and before the watchman opens the creaking doors, he is awakened by the call of the muezzin.

> It was during the reign of the Almohads, writes a chronicler, that, in its richness and splendour, Fez shone at its most magnificent. At that time, it was the most flourishing town in the Maghrib. In the reign of Al-Manṣūr and his followers there were in Fez seven hundred and eighty-five mosques and *zawiyas*—there are about two hundred and fifty today—two hundred and forty places of convenience and purification, and eighty public fountains, which were all fed with water from springs and brooks. There were ninety-three public baths and four hundred and seventy-two mills within and alongside the walls, not counting those outside the city. [The same chronicler goes on to mention eighty-nine thousand and thirty-six dwelling-houses; nineteen thousand and forty-one warehouses, four hundred and sixty-seven *funduqs* for the convenience of merchants, travellers, and the homeless; nine thousand and eighty-two shops, two commercial districts (*kaissariyas*), one in the Andalusian district, near the river Masmūda, and the other in the Kairuanese district; three thousand and sixty-four workshops, a hundred and seventeen public wash-houses; eighty-six tanneries; a hundred and sixteen dye-works; twelve coppersmitheries; a hundred and thirty-six bread-ovens, and eleven hundred and seventy other ovens.]
>
> Because of the proximity of the water, the dyeing establishments were set up on both sides of the tongue of land that splits the river Kebīr (the main river) from its point of entry into the town to as far as Rumīla. The bakers of doughnuts, fritters, and sweets, as well as those cooking gazelle and other meat, likewise had their little ovens in this district, and, on the storeys above them, the weavers and suppliers of dresses and cloaks were located . . .
>
> In Fez there were also four hundred paper-making shops, but they were all destroyed at the time of the famine, under the governments of Al-ᶜĀdil and his brothers, Al-Ma'mūn and Rashīd, during the years 618-638 (1221-1241 A.D.). These princes, who ruled during twenty years of misfortune and misery, were replaced by the Banū Merīn, who restored the country and re-established the safety of the highways . . .
>
> (*Rawḍ al-Qirṭās*)

The Merinids, who once again made Fez the imperial capital, also constructed, within its own walls, the royal city of New Fez (*Fās Jadīd*), to the west of the old city. This contained the sultan's palace with its courtyards, gardens and ponds

FAR LEFT: *Dye-vats near the river in Fez.*

and its population, which never really became urbanized, still retains in its memory the former military encampment.

THE JEWISH TOWN

Attached to the royal city of New Fez was the Jewish town, or Mellāh, for the court and the army had need of Jews as money-changers, bankers, and gold and silversmiths. Usury is forbidden to Muslims and the working of gold and silver is regarded as being not entirely without blame. The streets of the Mellāh have a different appearance from those of the Muslim town. The houses are distempered in blue, and wrought-iron windows and balconies are open to the street. One feels a certain Spanish influence, which dates back to the time when large numbers of Sephardic Jews had to flee the Inquisition and migrated to Morocco. The women wear gaudy head and neck scarves with fringes. Some of the older men still wear long black cowls. In earlier times, they were required to wear black as a distinguishing feature.

The Mellah always had its own administration: the town council—responsible to the Muslim administration of Fez—and a tribunal of rabbis fully empowered to give judgement on litigation between Jews, and for which the Muslim administration only provided the secular arm. And thus, within the walls of their town, the Jews lived in accordance with their own laws, in return for which they paid to the sultan a poll-tax, to which they were liable as 'protected persons' who were not obliged to render military service. As long as peace reigned, they enjoyed the protection of the sultanate; but when there was an overthrow of power, they were generally the first victims of acts of violence and plunder.

THE MADRASAS

It was also under the Merinids that the various *madrasas* in Fez were built. These were colleges, attached to the Qarawiyyīn University, which provided for the training of state officials. Up until a relatively recent period—the 1950s—these ancient *madrasas* still provided lodging for students from out of town. The institution of the *madrasa* comes from the East, from Khorāsān. It spread as far as Morocco, passing through Baghdad, Cairo and Tunis on the way. The *madrasa* is built around an inner courtyard, just like a dwelling-house, with the one difference that on at least one of its four sides the building consists of an open hall with a high ceiling, which is devoted to prayer and instruction. The building structure on the three other sides contains numerous cells where the students live. Every morning each student received a loaf of bread from one of the many mainmort foundations which, as anonymous benefactors, took care of the city.

MAINMORT FOUNDATIONS

The mainmort foundations, *ḥabūs*, to which a good part of the town and the surrounding gardens belong, are generally for the benefit of the Qarawiyyīn university, the mosques, the hospital, *māristān*, the Koran schools and the public baths. But there are also foundations dedicated to particular purposes such as, for example, the one whose purpose is to assure that the muezzins cry out from the top of the minarets between midnight and dawn when those afflicted with serious illnesses cannot sleep.

THE KORAN SCHOOLS

In every district there is a Koran school, where children of all ages learn the Koran by heart. This demands a great deal from the memory, and in the first instance all efforts are concentrated on this aspect alone. The teacher gives no explanations regarding the meaning of what is learnt by heart, and it is left to the linguistic intuition of the children gradually to understand the classical language which by its inflections is different from the simplified Moroccan dialect. The children learn the verses as if they were a kind of music. The literal meaning reveals itself to them only gradually, and they only understand the deeper meaning as the course of their life progresses, in accordance with their destiny, and depending on the spiritual or intellectual stimuli to which they are later exposed.

Since the professional requirements of the modern age make necessary a schooling in conformity with the European model, the Koran schools are more and more replaced by state institutions in which instruction is given in French as well as in Arabic, and a shift towards the modern style of education inevitably takes place. And thus a profound alteration in the mentality and way of thinking is brought about.

ADMINISTRATION

Modern historians are astonished that such a large city, which seldom comprised less than a hundred thousand souls, could always be administered by so few officials. The city is governed by a representative of the sultan, known today as the pasha, to whom are responsible the officials *muqaddamūn* in charge of each district. The pasha himself acts as judge with regard to breaches of public order, and he is assisted by the chief judge of the city *qāḍī al-quḍā* who, as supreme head of the university and trustee of all mainmort foundations, possess a special and scarcely less powerful, position: he is as it were, the spokesman for the assembly of learned doctors, whose function it is to guard and interpret the law.

Islamic jurisprudence starts from the premiss that outward and visible misdemeanours must be quickly and condignly punished, so as to preserve the social order, but it does not seek to investigate by all means transgressions whose ill effects cannot be compensated for. In such cases, neither confession nor witness is sought after. The guilty party, it is said, will ineluctably have to settle his account with God. This rule, which European influence has diluted, protects the court from judicial error, and also from pronouncing on ultimate guilt, by relying on an inevitably insufficient, because only too human, psychology.

Next in authority to the chief judge, comes the overseer of markets, *muḥtasib*, who determines the basic prices, judges disputes between merchants, and to whom the trustees (*'umanā*), of the individual guilds have to give account.

In principle, taxes are supposed to be taken from the *zakāt* tithe which every Muslim is required to give yearly out of his harvest, increase in flocks, or monetary gains, for the benefit of the poor, the debtors, the homeless, and the 'combatants in the way of God' (members of spiritual orders who have dedicated themselves to poverty). The sultan had the right to collect this tithe to support the holy war (*jihād*) that is to say, warfare exclusively for the defence of the religious community. Supplementary levies, which numerous sultans imposed on the people, arbitrarily or driven by necessity, were always considered unjust, and were the most frequent cause of uprisings.

The three high officials—the city governor or pasha, the chief judge, and the overseer of markets—employed the services of a few clerks, and had at their command a small body of guardians. This was the total officialdom. And yet, apart from occasional disorders, this large city lived mostly in peace. This was only possible because, although not 'organized' it nevertheless consisted of truly organic units, for each activity still retained a simple and intelligible meaning with regard to the whole: like the sand on a river-bed, that takes on the shape of the waves flowing over it, the collectivity was capable of ordering itself anew, after every and any ripple, in accordance with universally understood prototypes.

CRAFTSMANSHIP

In Fez, craftsmanship still retains something of its ancient meaning; it corresponds to a necessity, and at the same time is an art. The heads of trustees of the various guilds ensure that the work of each master conforms to the required standard of excellence, that the materials used are of good quality, and that prices are just; they also provide for the sick and needy members of their professional community. But today the guilds are threatened by modern economy and driven into a tight corner by the political trade unions; if they should ever disappear, something much more than a particular outward expression of professional solidarity would be lost.

I knew a comb-maker who worked in the street of his guild, the *mashshāṭīn*. He was called ᶜAbd al-ᶜAzīz ('slave of the Almighty'), and always wore a black *jellāba*—the loose, hooded garment with sleeves—and a white turban with the *lithām*, the face veil, which surrounded his somewhat severe features. He obtained the horn for his combs from ox skulls, which he bought from butchers. He dried the horned skulls at a rented place, removed the horns, opened them lengthwise, and straightened them over a fire, a procedure that had to be done with the greatest care, lest they should break. From this raw material he cut combs and turned boxes for antimony (used as an eye decoration) on a simple lathe; this he did by manipulating with his left hand a bow which, wrapped round a spindle, caused the apparatus to rotate. In his right hand he held the knife, and with his foot he pushed against the counter-weight. As he worked he would sing Koranic *sūras* in a humming tone.

I learned that as a result of an eye disease which is common in Africa, he was already half blind and that, in view of long practice, he was able to 'feel' his work rather than see it. One day he complained to me that the importation of plastic combs was diminishing his business: 'It is not only a pity that today, solely on account of price, poor quality combs from a factory are being preferred to much more durable horn combs,' he said; 'it is also senseless that

Tailor at work in the Old City.

One of the many traditional crafts still practised in Morocco.

people should stand by a machine and mindlessly repeat the same movement, while an old craft like mine falls into oblivion. My work may seem crude to you; but it harbours a subtle meaning which cannot be explained in words. I myself acquired it only after many long years, and even if I wanted to, I could not automatically pass it on to my son, if he himself did not wish to acquire it—and I think he would rather take up another occupation. This craft can be traced back from apprentice to master until one reaches our Lord Seth, the son of Adam. It was he who first taught it to men, and what a Prophet brings—for Seth was a Prophet—must clearly have a special purpose, both outwardly and inwardly. I gradually came to understand that there is nothing fortuitous about this craft, that each movement and each procedure is the bearer of an element of wisdom. But not everyone can understand this. But even if one does not know this, it is still stupid and reprehensible to rob men of the inheritance of Prophets, and to put them in front of a machine where, day in and day out, they must perform a meaningless task.'

Consequently, the dire straits in which Moroccan craftsmanship finds itself is not merely an outward predicament, but above all a spiritual threat. Even if not every Arab craftsman has as much understanding of his craft as our comb-maker, nevertheless most professions still have a spiritual content, which will progressively disappear with the innovation of modern industry.

Even the water-carriers, who do nothing else but fill their tarred goatskins at the public fountains in order to offer a cool drink to thirsty people in the market-place, indifferent as to whether they receive a voluntary token or nothing at all, show in their demeanour a human dignity, such as, in European countries, the sower may still have, as he contemplatively scatters his seed.

Even the beggars, who squat outside the mosques and on the bridges and who reveal their profession by their much-patched garments, do not make their request with shame, but cry: 'Give what is God's!' or intone to themselves in a monotonous voice a pious refrain.

For almost everyone who has not been sucked into the whirlpool of the modern world lives his life here as if it were something provisional which does not definitively engage his soul, but which belongs to the 'Divina Commedia' of earthly existence.

If one should escape from the throng of the bazaars, and enter one of the high, narrow, ravine-like streets, above which the heavens peep down between the high black walls of houses, and where, in the half-light, a few people are passing—a woman, perhaps, wrapped up in white flowing garments, grave-faced men or a beautiful child—one encounters the cool, fine breath of ephemerality, which belongs to every truly Islamic city. Everywhere, in the midst of sound buildings, there are ruins, which no one takes amiss, for death belongs to life; even new buildings seem, under their white lime plaster, to be timeless. Over everything lies the 'shroud of Islam', as Pierre Loti called it; over everything, indeed, lies a reflection of the Koranic verse: *Everything on earth shall pass away; there remaineth but the face of thy Lord resplendent with Majesty and Bounty.*

Thus to the extent that the Islamic city remains faithful to tradition, it has something monastic about it: the men are all covered in the same cowls, and go through the streets, not like native townsmen, but like eternal wanderers. The women are veiled, anonymous and withdrawn from public curiosity. The houses have no windows to the outside. There is no such thing as a tavern.

THE MOSQUES

Every now and again the otherwise unbroken wall permits us a glimpse into the interior of a mosque, which is composed of large halls grouped around a courtyard, the proportions of which exhale peace and unity. In the middle of the courtyard a fountain gushes from a shallow basin and sparkles in the sun. Round about, on the rows of arches, the sunlight trickles over the arabesques and glistens like dew. In the halls, where honey-coloured matting stretches as far as eye can see, we find the gentle complement to the courtyard. This is the place that offers rest to the 'wayfarer' (*ibn as-sabīl*).

As one wanders through the narrow streets, one may suddenly hear above the roof-tops the long drawn out call of the muezzin, who begins his call at the top of his voice, and then gradually lets it fade away in more ringing tones. He makes his call to the four directions, one after the other: east, north, west and south: 'God is most great! God is most great! I bear witness that there is no divinity but God. I bear witness that Muḥammad is the Messenger of God. Come to prayer! Come to salvation! God is most great! God is most great!' In the distance other muezzins echo the call, and the air is filled with their soaring, plaintive song.

Immediately the townspeople leave their work and close their shops, and hurry towards the mosques.

At the fountain in the courtyard, those who have not already made their ablution wash their face, hands and feet, and then form up in rows behind the officiant (*imām*), who stands in the prayer-niche *mihrāb* his face turned towards Mecca.

He begins the prayer by raising both his hands, pronounces the words 'God is most great!' and brings his hands down again. Then he recites the 'opening' chapter, *Fātiḥa*, of the Koran:

In the Name of God, the Clement, the Merciful:
Praise be to God the Lord of the worlds,
The Clement, the Merciful,
The owner of the Day of Judgement,
Thee do we worship and in Thee do we seek refuge.
Guide us upon the straight path,
The path of those to whom Thou art gracious,
Not of those on whom Thine anger hath fallen,
Nor of those who go astray.

To this central Islamic prayer the worshipper then adds a further *sūra*, or extract, of his own choosing, such as the following:

By the brightness of day,
And by the night when it falleth,
Thy Lord hath not forsaken thee, nor doth He hate thee,
And verily the next world will be better for thee than this one,
And verily thy Lord will give unto thee so that thou wilt be content.
Did He not find thee an orphan and protect thee?
Did He not find thee wandering and direct thee?
Did He not find thee destitute and enrich thee?
Therefore the orphan oppress not,
Therefore the beggar turn not away,
Therefore of the bounty of thy Lord be thy discourse. (Koran 93:1–11)

Then he makes a forward inclination, while saying the words 'God is most great'; he returns to the erect position, and makes a prostration, touching the ground twice with his forehead. One of those praying behind him makes the responses aloud, while the others follow the movements of worship silently. The whole cycle is repeated the prescribed number of times. At the end, all those who have been praying sit down side by side in rows. They then recite the profession of faith, pronounce the greeting 'peace be upon you', and finally, with their hands raised, silently make their personal prayers.

Between dawn and nightfall this act of prayer is repeated five times. It thus regulates and determines the nature of the whole day. If the worshipper is unable to go to a mosque, he performs the prayer at home or in the fields, either alone or in a group, or as the officiant for his own family; for in Islam there is no ordained clergy to perform the rites. An officiant is required only to have a proper knowledge of the forms of worship and to lead an upright life.

The regularity of the rites and the fact that their outward form is prescribed down to the smallest detail means that the life of all believers is penetrated by a common spiritual vibration, one which is nourished in space and time by a constantly repeated act of the will. It confers on everyone a particular inward attitude, which shows itself outwardly in various ways, not the least of which is a deep-seated courtesy that is common to rich and poor, cultivated and uncultivated alike.

This is the form or spiritual style that makes tolerable any misery that may occur in a city such as Fez, and keeps in check all human excesses. If this form should ever be destroyed—and the meretricious propaganda of the modern world, with every technological means at its disposal, has already made serious inroads—all that would be left in the alleyways and streets of the old city would be the misery and ugliness of the masses struggling for their daily bread.

THE RACES

For the European who encounters the Moroccan populace for the first time, the multiplicity of racial and psychological types present within it is overshadowed by a striking similarity of facial expression, stemming from Islamic values, which appears to him as a sort of mask. Upon closer acquaintance,

A man of the Kabyle with a child.

however, he discovers that the spiritual attitude, compounded of dignity and resignation, which this expression reflects, has nothing mask-like about it, for the almost somnolent restfulness of the faces can readily manifest both spontaneity of feeling and shrewdness of understanding. Conversely, from the point of view of a Moroccan of the old school, European faces, with their tenseness, hyperactivity, and self-consciousness, have something malevolent about them.

This at first sight striking similarity of expression has nothing racial about it, however, since in the population of a city like Fez there is not only a mixture of Arab, Berber and Moorish blood: slaves of both sexes brought from the Sudan have provided a Negro contribution to the mixture; Jews converted to Islam have married into old Fez families; and with the flight of the Moriscos from Spain, an Iberian element was also added.

The Negro contribution is always clearly recognizable. On the other hand,

Arabs and Berbers, who both belong to the white race, are not easy to distinguish, although there are a number of so-called regional types which are characteristically Arab or Berber. As Semites, the Arabs generally have oval faces and lively features; when they are lean, they resemble sparrowhawks; and amongst them one also encounters massive Assyrian heads. The Berbers, on the other hand, have prominent and angular cheek-bones, short noses, and somewhat prominent mouths. This type is especially common amongst the Kabyles of the Rif, a group that constitutes one of the ethnic reservoirs of Fez, as is also Tafilelt, a Berber region situated in the Saharan axis of the city. Compared with the more mobile Semitic features, the Berbers have a rock-like

A Berber youth.

appearance, as if they were carved out of basalt; perhaps it is only the implacable mountain landscape that is reflected in their features. Also typical of the Berbers is an elongated skull that reminds one of ancient Egyptian sculptures. In the city all these various races, Berbers, Arabs, and Negroes are combined with the Moors, a light-skinned mixed race that has received contributions from Iberian Phoenicians, Romans and Greeks of the African colonies, and other peoples. They are present as a merchant caste in all the larger cities of the Maghrib.

CITY DWELLERS AND BEDOUINS

Quite apart from the fact that the race of the city dwellers is much less unmixed than that of the country people, the Bedouin is distinguishable from the city dweller by his striking bearing; he is in all respects a more homogeneous type. Ibn Khaldūn was right: in the town there is every possible human type, from the refined scholar and skilful craftsman to the bloated glutton and the grotesque clown who lives on the charity of those whom he makes to laugh. Amongst the townsfolk human diversity reveals itself as a fan of possibilities that is much more extensive than in the case of the Bedouins, and it does this in both a good and a bad sense. The hard but natural life of the *fellāḥ* and the nomad is conducive neither to formal refinement nor to human degeneration.

The city dweller has a slight contempt for the untutored countryman, and while the latter may admire the former, at the same time he despises him as a weakling and mistrusts him as a merchant. Masculine dignity and beauty are more often to be found among the Bedouins than among the townspeople, and this difference has become more pronounced since traditional masculine dress in the towns has increasingly been replaced by European clothes.

In Fez one can find small spice-merchants, who are recognizable by their indigo-blue garments. They come from the Anti-Atlas, a chain of mountains that protects the Sūs from the Sahara. Many of them are from the Haratīn, a people of elegant stature characterized by an olive-brown skin and mongoloid features. According to some ethnologists they derive from an ancient mixture of Berbers and Negroes; according to others they are a people that migrated from Asia to the northern Sahara. With extreme frugality and industriousness these merchants save money with which they maintain their families in the far-off south and with which, at an advanced age, they may build themselves a fine house in their stark and rocky homeland.

To the same race belong the travelling apothecaries and medical practitioners who display in the marketplace their herbs, powders, and dried lizards, and impassively await clients. It has happened that European travellers, unable to obtain alternative medical assistance, have had recourse to their ministrations, and have been astonished at the rapidity of the cure.

The porters and messengers, who can be seen waiting in grey burnouses in the square of the carpenters (*an-najjārīn*), come from the Middle Atlas. They are Berbers from the Zerzai tribe.

SOCIAL CLASSES

Although in Islam there are no hereditary castes, the *shurafā'* (plural of *sharīf*) or descendants of the Prophet nevertheless represent a kind of sacred aristrocracy, for they are regarded as the bearers of a special blessing.

> 'One of the advantages of the city of Fez',writes al-Kattānī 'is that so many families of *shurafā'* are present within it to a degree scarcely found in any other city . . . The *shurafā'* are the ornaments and the stars of the world. Thanks to them, both land and people are protected against trials and misfortunes . . .' (*Salwāt al-Anfās*)

The descendance of this nobility is usually considered authentic only in the male line, which goes back either to Ḥasan or Ḥusain, the two sons of Fāṭima, Muḥammad's daughter. In Fez the Idrīsid-Ḥasanid *shurafā'* are numerous, and often impoverished. Nevertheless, at certain periods, especially since the decline of the western caliphate, they have fulfilled the role of a true élite. In the sixteenth, seventeenth and eighteenth centuries, Fez was spiritually dominated by a few *shurafā'* families, namely the Idrīsids, the Wazzānī, and Saqallī, the Fāsī, the Kattānī, and others, from amongst whom many scholars, judges, and Sufi masters originated. As their outward power increased, the heirs of these families yielded more and more to the temptation of basking in the fame of their predecessors. As a result, the true spiritual succession constantly shifted from the principal to the secondary branches of these families.

In every traditional culture, there are, for every professional activity and social class, specific models or prototypes, the formative power of which remains effective only for as long as the whole culture remains true to itself. In the Islamic world, one particular model of this kind is that of the scholar, who knows the revealed law; another is that of the noble and generous leader, and not less important is the model of the patriarch or elder, whose age confers on him a certain wisdom and dignity. It can truly be said that the Arabo-Islamic civilization only degenerates to the extent that it disregards these models or prototypes.

Ibn Khaldūn calls commerce an ignoble and unmanly activity, and this is all the more plausible in that in all the towns along the southern and eastern coasts of the Mediterranean there is a particular type of sly and greedy merchant. Nevertheless commerce—or 'buying and selling', as the Arabs call it—also offers the possibility of a spiritual attitude in conformity with Islam, and this consists in accepting gains and losses with equal equanimity—an attitude that is incompatible with deception. It must not be forgotten that the Prophet himself was a merchant in his youth.

I knew in Fez a rich and charitable merchant, who looked on the world with a contemplative disdain. His business consisted of an entirely empty shop, in the *sūq al-bālī* where each evening blankets and clothing were auctioned. He used to observe this lively and noisy spectacle with the look of a falcon reposing on a branch. Only now and again would he give a sign to a boy who stood in front of his shop, whereupon the boy would quickly dive into the mêlée, make a bid, and secure a purchase.

THE TOMBS

One of the last books written and printed in Fez before the arrival of the French bore the title 'The consolation of souls and the true histories of the sages and saints buried in Fez'. In this book, the author, Muḥammad ben Jaᶜfar ben Idrīs al-Kattānī, supplies short biographies of over a thousand men and women, arranged according to the districts and streets in which their graves are to be found. Fez thus takes on the appearance of a vast mausoleum. 'In Fez,' runs a proverb, 'there is not a square yard of ground that was not inhabited by a saint.' The kingdom of the dead is greater by far than the kingdom of the living.

Graveyard shrouded in mist on the outskirts of Fez.

The tomb-speckled hills to the north of Fez, with their little valleys, their caves, and their ruins, are the refuge of the colourful travelling people, composed of jugglers, fortune-tellers, jesters, beggars, and prostitutes, who had their own district in every medieval town.

THE MADMEN

The traditional world does not exclude unusual or downright bizarre individuals, who are part of nature and inevitable. The Moroccan people are tolerant of harmless idiots, and may even show them a certain respect, in that, like children and sacred animals, they may sometimes be the bearers of certain spiritual influences, just as criminal madmen may easily become the instruments of diabolic forces. Beneficent madmen are often attracted by holy places, like mediums who physically assimilate the special blessing of these places, and put themselves under its protection.

THE FOOLS OF GOD

One must also reckon with the possibility that an apparent madman is in reality a *majdhūb*, one 'attracted by God', whose reason has so to speak been over-powered by a spiritual drunkenness, so that he forgets his surroundings, and 'feels neither hot nor cold'.

There are also dervishes who use the mask of madness in order to be able to live alone in the midst of the world and be free from all social fetters. To such a category belonged Mulay aṣ-Ṣiddīq, who died around 1939. He came from a distinguished Fez family and, as a young man, had embarked on a promising career as a lawyer, when he met a Sufi master who wandered through the land as a 'fool of God'. He became his disciple and adopted the same way of life. When he heard that his brother had spoken of him with rage and disgust, he visited his house at a moment when no one was in, and washed the floors of each room with his own hands. Thereafter his relatives left him in peace.

Most of the time he travelled. When, however, he visited Fez, he installed himself in a small cemetery that abutted on the house in which I was living at that time. The cemetery was completely full of graves, and surrounded by a wall. A tall, lonely palm-tree grew in one corner, and along one of the sides stood a half-ruined row of pillars, in front of which the strange man had stretched out a mat with which to shelter his wife and children. In these surroundings, which reminded me of the old masters' renderings of the Adoration of the Magi, he would receive his disciples, mostly poor and uneducated people, but occasionally also people from the higher classes.

Every morning it was his practice to wander through the market with his most faithful disciples, chanting the profession of faith 'there is no divinity but God', and receiving alms. He wore an enormous rosary, with beads as big as apples, that was wound twice around his neck and hung down over his heavy round body. He supported himself on a staff. His somewhat Mongoloid and impenetrable face was surmounted by a massive blue-green turban. Behind him always walked a herculean, one-eyed son of the desert, who was dressed only in loosely stitched-together pieces of leather that scarcely covered his brown muscles. One might have taken him for a highwayman, had it not been for the child-like look of benevolence in his single eye. It was he who carried the bag for alms.

Sometimes the group would enter a house where a festivity, a wedding or a circumcision, was in progress. The men would sit down in a circle in the courtyard; and when, as was the custom, the host served tea, Mulay aṣ-Ṣiddīq would take the copper tray used to carry the tea-glasses and the hammer used to break the sugar and, beginning to sing a mystical song, he would use these utensils as ear-splitting cymbals. His disciples would then rise, take each other by the hand, and, chanting the Name of God, they would begin to dance. I myself was once witness when aged men suffering from the palsy, who had followed the outlandish master with the greatest of difficulty, suddenly threw away their crutches and, as if transported, threw themselves into the dance. When finally Mulay aṣ-Ṣiddīq stopped the dance and everyone sat down, women who had watched the scene from the flat roof, threw down money and jewelry with jubilant cries.

When the alms bag was full, couscous, meat, and vegetables would be bought, and, in the cemetery that the group used as a meeting place, a large meal would be prepared on an open fire, to which all the poor of the district were invited.

Mulay aṣ-Ṣiddīq would accept no disciple who did not put at his disposal all that he possessed. Sometimes the master would return a part of this to him, so that he might fulfill his commitments. Everything else was given to the poor.

This 'fool of God' was a source of embarrassment to the educated; the middle classes looked on him with a mixture of benevolence and amusement. But many poor people, porters, day labourers, and donkey drivers, as well as not a few craftsmen, and even some educated men and women, venerated him so much that in his presence, they behaved like timid children.

THE SEPULCHRAL MOSQUE OF IDRIS II

Just as the sepulchral mosque of Idrīs I on Mount Zerhūn may be said to be the heart of the whole of Morocco, so the sanctuary enclosing the tomb of Idrīs II, both by its situation and by its meaning, is the heart of Fez. Here, in the pillared halls around the sun-drenched courtyard, travellers and pilgrims find rest, and in the great hall that contains the tomb, the elders of the various families gather in the evenings. Certain modern historians question whether Idrīs II is really buried here. It was only in the fourteenth century, when the floor of the mosque was being renewed, that an uncorrupted body was found, and assumed to be that of the founder of the city. The citizens of Fez, however, have no doubts about the authenticity of the tomb. For them it has been confirmed by a thousand miracles and is clearly perceptible in the spiritual power that continues to emanate from the sacred place. A mystic of the eighteenth century, Ḥammū ben Rahmūn, wrote: 'I have never passed close to this place without feeling the poignant longing which emanates from his tomb, and which lays hold on me like death, so much do I venerate his awesome greatness.'

Once a year the guilds and brotherhoods offer their homage to Mulay Idrīs. The solemn procession is headed by the silk-weavers, who make the brocaded cloth, covered with Koranic verses, which will be the new covering for the tomb. The coppersmiths bring an immense incense burner. The merchants and stonemasons from the Sahara approach the sanctuary to the beating of low-sounding drums, and sacrifice an ox, the meat from which will be distributed to the impoverished descendants of the saint. In the past, before 1930, members of the ʿIsāwā *tarīqa* used to make their way along the main streets, dancing ecstatically, until they reached the tomb. The incantatory sound of their flutes mingled with the jubilant cries of the women who looked down on them from the edges of the roof-tops.

To end this chapter, I shall reproduce an inscription which I found on a house in Fez. It expresses very well the Islamic attitude that has often been described as fatalism, as if an awareness of the pre-determined nature of all human endeavour could possibly deter initiative. A man of the people said to me that the original text of this inscription had been written by the hand of an angel on a rock near Jerusalem:

> In the Name of God, the Clement, the Merciful: remember My loving-kindness towards thee, when thou wast still a droplet, and forget not how I shaped thee when thou wast still in thy mother's womb. Thou camest into the world defenceless and innocent, and I provided for thee from whence thou knewest not. Therefore trust in Me completely in whatever thou doest or leavest undone. I will be thy sufficiency, whatever be thy fear or thy care. Commit thine actions to Me, and know that I make known My commandments, and do what I will. (*Salwāt al-Anfās*)

5 The House

THE TRUE, unveiled face of Fez remains hidden to whoever knows Fez only from the street, and has seen only the shopping alleyways and the grey outer walls of the houses. The inside of the house is the strongly defended domain of the women. The expression 'harem' (from the Arabic *ḥaram*), which has entered the English language, means nothing other than 'sanctuary'.

When one is invited to be a guest in a house in Fez, the master of the house, after he has taken his guest through the small outside door into a dark L-shaped corridor, goes a few steps ahead, and makes a sign to the women who may be in the house, so that they may withdraw. They thus vacate the inner courtyard, to which the corridor leads, and from which one gains access to the surrounding rooms. As soon as the guests have sat down in one of these rooms, the hand of a servant draws the curtain over the door, so that only a small section of the courtyard remains visible to the male guests, and the coming and going of the women, their serving of any refreshments, or their play, is perceptible only by the clinking of their bracelets and the sound of their footsteps on the tiles. Only relatives or close friends of the family are permitted to see the women occupants of the house, although the strictness of this custom has now been greatly eased.

In the reception room, low divans are generally situated along the three walls that face the courtyard, and the floor is covered with mats or carpets. The rooms are high, so that they retain a certain coolness. The ceiling, hidden high in darkness, rests on black cedar beams. All the light comes from the courtyard. It is only rarely that a room on an upper storey has a window to the outside.

In the houses in which the Moroccan style of living has been maintained, the rooms have virtually no furniture, apart from divans and a few wall shelves. Furniture is indeed superfluous, in that one removes one's shoes or slippers on entering the rooms, and in that one takes one's food, with carefully washed hands, from a common serving dish. Through this simplicity of life, and through the modest dignity that comes from the prescribed prayers, the differences of social class are greatly attenuated. In the house of a Fez scholar, or of a well-to-do bourgeois, one can find eating together men of the most varied social standing. The master mason who has been repairing the roof, the tenant who on his mule has just brought his landlord his rent in the shape of a load of wheat from his farm, and even the beggar who enjoys the favour of the house, all behave with the same tact as the educated friends of the host.

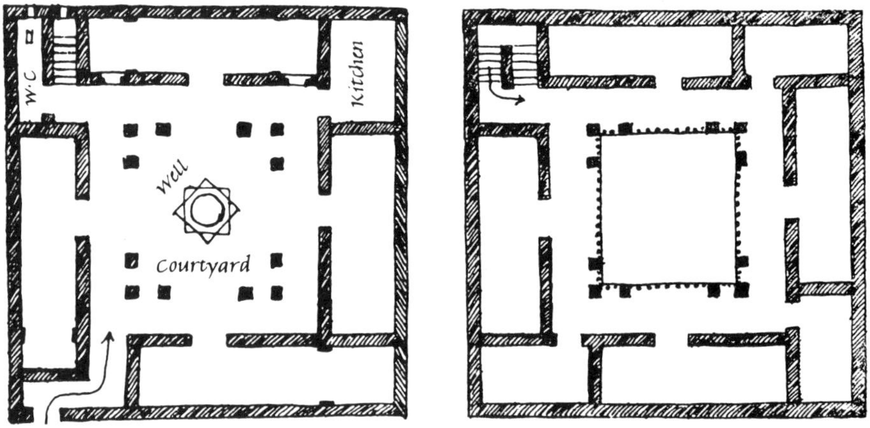

Plan of the upper and lower storeys of a typical house.

The kitchen in which the women prepare the meal is also as simple as can be. Most often the stove is no more than a small clay structure which is filled with wood and can be placed anywhere. People sleep on the low divans lining the walls. One can sleep, wrapped in one's mantle, in the same place as one was seated during the day. All the modalities of living, to the extent that European influence has not yet had an effect, retain something of the way of the nomad who, at any moment, is able to load his entire household onto a beast of burden, and leave the area.

And yet the inhabitants of Fez knew a certain luxury in living. Leo Africanus, a Moroccan who in the sixteenth century was taken to Rome as a prisoner, wrote about Fez as follows:

> The houses of this city are built either of brick or of well-chiselled stone. Most of them are very beautiful, and are decorated with mosaics. Following ancient custom, the open courtyards or halls are covered with glazed tiles, brightly coloured in a manner reminiscent of majolica. The inhabitants also have the custom of covering the ceilings with beautiful ornamentation in rich colours such as gold and silver. The buildings commonly have two or even three storeys, with balconies or arcades permitting easy passage from one room to the next, for the middle of the house is open, and the rooms face each other over the courtyard. The

doors are very broad and high, and those who can afford it have them made out of carved wood. They also equip their rooms with cupboards made of the finest wood. These may extend from one wall to the other, and are used to store all manner of precious things . . . The arcades of the houses are supported either on brick pillars, covered with majolica to half way up, or on marble pillars; and the arches themselves are covered with mosaics. The beams which rest on the pillars and which bear the weight of the uppper storeys are of wood, and are carefully and artistically decorated with brightly coloured carvings.

In many houses there are open pools, usually rectangular in shape, five to six ells wide, ten to twelve ells long, and three or four feet deep. These are decorated round their edges with majolica. On the short sides, are similarly decorated fountains which feed the pools. These pools are always very clean, but they are only used in summer, since that is when the women and children like to bathe and swim in them.

There is also the custom of constructing on the roof of the house an observation tower with a comfortable room, where the women, when they are tired of sewing and knitting, can amuse themselves, since, owing to the height of these towers, it is possible to survey the whole extent of the city, with its seven hundred or so oratories and fifty large mosques . . .

(*Leo Africanus*)

Looking through to the inner courtyard of a traditional house.

HOUSE CONSTRUCTION

When a house is built, the architect erects the walls, the rooms around the inner courtyard, the arcades that border the rooms of the upper storey, and the stairway leading up to them. Only when his work is finished do the various craftsmen come to cover the floors and pillars with coloured tiles, to embellish the door-niches and arches with stucco honeycombs and arabesques, and to carve and paint the woodwork. In this division of labour one sees the dual presence of the sedentary culture and the nomadic heritage, which Ibn Khaldūn considered to be decisive for the Maghrib and the whole of the Islamic world. The ornamentation of a building recalls the wall hangings and curtains of a nomadic tent. Their compatibility with architecture lies in their geometrical style which, precisely, is natural both to the crystalline character of architecture and to the archaic ornamental art of the Bedouins. The city culture has absorbed the Bedouin heritage and brought it to fruition spiritually. The rigorously geometrical reticulations and rosettes, which cover the walls of buildings like hoar-frost or like star-worlds, are for the Moorish artist a symbol of the everywhere discernible unity of God.

THE ART OF ORNAMENTATION

The artist or craftsman who produces the wall mosaics begins by drawing his design on a large sheet of paper. Then, with his pointed hammer, he cuts out the necessary individual elements from coloured ceramic tiles, carefully arranges these on top of the design on his sheet of paper, which is now laid out on the

Intricate zellij wall mosaic in geometrical design.

ground, and finally applies the pieces to the wall, which has been freshly covered with mortar. In these mosaics the colour blue is predominant; this is in order to confer on the space an impression of freshness and coolness, as in a shady oasis. Purplish blue, emerald green, cherry red, and ochre—these are the commonest colours. The favourite design is 'God's spider's web', the very name of which evokes the 'miracle of the spider': When the Prophet, to escape his persecutors, fled from Mecca, he and his companion Abū Bakr hid for three days and three nights in a cave. The hostile Meccans rode out in search of them, and on the first morning they reached the entrance to the cave. But a spider had spun its net across it, a dove had laid its eggs on the threshold, and a wild rose-bush had stretched out its blossoming branches, so that the pursuers thought that no one could possibly have recently entered the cave. The mosaic spider's web, however, resembles its model only remotely. It is in fact a geometrical rosette, which begins as a star and then extends outwards in interlacing bands, that follow a rigorous plan, and form a rich and extensive network. Several such complete designs can intertwine with one another on one surface, and then they form, especially when they originate in stars with varying numbers of rays, a shimmering planetarium, in which each line starts from a centre and leads to a centre, a motif that once again strongly evokes the Islamic idea of omnipresent unity. 'In relation to the Divine Unicity', wrote the Arab mystic ʿAbd al-Karīm al-Jīlī, 'the possibilities that constitute the world are mirrors that reflect one another, so that in each individual mirror everything that is contained in the others is reflected in the particular way that corresponds to the mirror in question'.

The same geometrical networks can also be executed in stucco. Since, at one time, I wished to learn the Moorish art of stucco, I offered myself as an apprentice to a master who lived in Fez. In my support, I said that I already had a steady hand in the working of plaster, and that I possessed a certain facility in the reproduction of forms. By way of testing me, he enquired what I would propose to do if, for example, he asked me to ornament a rectangular piece of wall of such and such a size. I outlined how I would cover the area with a vegetable arabesque, and fill in the empty spaces with animals such as gazelles, birds and other creatures. 'No', he said, 'that would not be worth much. Birds, horses, weasels and other quadrupeds are to be found everywhere. One only has to look around and imitate. That requires no knowledge. But if I say to you, deploy four rosettes (*tasāṭir*), beginning alternately in an eight-ray and in a ten-ray star, so that side by side, and leaving no spaces, they fill the entire wall, that would be a different matter. And that is art!'

The artists who ornament buildings with stucco cut the designs into the freshly applied plaster, which is then hardened with lime-water, so that it will resist all weathers for centuries.

The honeycomb forms (*muqarnas*), by means of which one can make a multi-vaulted transition from one flat surface to another, and of which the stalactites in niches and arches are also made, are first poured out individually, and later assembled together. Their basic element is a wedge which supports the corners of a cupola that sits on a rectangular base. By superimposing several of these wedges, one obtains a sort of honeycomb, which seems to grow out of the flat wall and which supports an overhanging part of the building. If one allows the sides of a few of these wedges to stand free, they hang down like stalactites from the arch from which they themselves form. The play of light on the variously inclined surfaces gives the stucco a wonderful and almost translucent quality.

It was during the reign of the Merinids, when many Andalusian artists emigrated to Morocco, that it began to be the custom to cover the walls with stucco, and to work this stucco at different levels, so that the ornamentation seemed to consist of several superimposed layers of reticulated patterns. In this way the walls lose their heaviness. They seem to become as light as a tent, and yet look as if they were made of rock crystal.

In the reign of the Saadians who were, so to speak, the cultural heirs of Granada, walls that looked as if they had been spun out of light were supported on the finest of pillars, so that they no longer seemed to weigh upon the ground, but rather to hang down like a curtain of pearls. The contrast between the white stucco and the dark cedar beams, which gives Moroccan architecture its particular charm, was consciously used to produce a luminous coolness, like that of snow in the moonlight.

The ornaments carved out of stucco are not all purely geometrical. There is also the vegetable arabesque. This however does not follow a natural model but obeys only its own rhythmic law.

Of the highest perfection are the inscriptions—either engraved in stucco, carved in wood, or chiselled in ceramic tiles—for calligraphy was not only the affair of the craftsman: it was also practised by many learned people and even by sultans. Something of the holiness of the Koranic words passes over into the writing that embodies them. As with the Jews and the Christian monks of earlier times, the copying of the revealed Book is a work of sanctification. Moroccan handwriting has preserved a relatively Arab style, one that is more hieratic than the so-called 'eastern' style. The calligraphers, however, had not one but many styles at their disposal and, depending on which one they used, could give to the inscription either a flowing or a static quality.

In addition to cupolas of masonry, one also finds in Morocco roofs of cedarwood, which from the inside look like polyhedra and outside are covered with green-glazed tiles. The painting of roofs, doors, and caskets involves not only geometrical figures, but also light garlands in which sometimes a Turkish influence can be discerned. The art of coloured pottery, which flourishes in Fez to this day, transposes the geometrical models, in conformity with the round shape of plates and vases, into undulant and circular patterns.

FAR RIGHT: *Exquisitely carved muqarnas ceiling of stucco and cedarwood.*

Arches surround a courtyard.

FAR LEFT:
Detail of Koranic inscriptions in the ᶜAttārīn Madrasah.

The absence of pictorial representation from Moorish art does not mean that it is unaware of the symbolic value of natural phenomena. On the contrary, all natural phenomena are recognized as 'signs' of God, and this is why man must not seek to imitate them. Art must remain within its own domain. Only then is it in conformity with Divine Law.

One day, in order to record the various racial types that I had observed in Fez, I modelled a number of heads. When I took these to a potter for firing, the master potter looked at them disapprovingly one after the other, and said, 'God has created us out of the same clay as these pots, but man makes pots and God makes men. Wilt thou then imitate God, and make His works laughable?'

There are buildings—and they are amongst the most beautiful—whose only decoration consists of arcades around their courtyards. Islamic art is particularly sensitive to the nobility of an arch. What a Moorish arch expresses lies not so much in its light bearing as in its shape. It confers a special quality on the empty space that it surrounds. One might even say that it is only thanks to the arch that space, which in itself is endless and unqualified, can reveal the quality inherent in it. The circle traced by the horse-shoe arch makes space the centre. The pointed summit, like the flame of a candle, gives it its ascending tendency, while the rectangular framework, slightly in relief, which sometimes surrounds the arch, establishes an equilibrium between the outward-expanding curvature and the cubic nature of the building itself. A work of this kind is free from all human contingency. It pertains to a sort of visual mathematics, and thereby it satisfies the contemplative intellect. It is like a sacred formula, whose content is never exhausted, or like the life-giving jet of water that gushes from the fountain in the courtyard.

Such a severe architecture has need in fact of the playing of water, and the liberating presence of trees and bushes in flower, in the secret world of its courtyard, so that this may be entirely transformed into a cool oasis.

Sometimes the courtyard extends into an enclosed garden (*rawḍ*), only one or two sides of which are lined with living accommodation, the remaining sides being bounded by high walls. Often, as in medieval cloisters, a pillared ambulatory surrounds the courtyard or garden. The inner garden is built in accordance with an architectural plan: between the elevated pathways, geometrically shaped recipients are filled with earth. In contrast to this orderly plan, the trees and bushes are allowed to grow freely. If possible, one or several plants of every species is planted, just as, in a Persian miniature, every species existing in nature is represented by one example. Through the middle of the garden flow canals with trickling water.

MARRIAGE

The square shape of most Arab houses, with a room on each of the four sides, corresponds to the Islamic law of marriage, according to which a man may have

The secret world of the courtyard.

Moroccan bride.

four wives. The man must provide living quarters for each wife, and must devote an equal amount of time and attention to all. He is the guest of his wives, and every night must be put up by one of them in turn, unless by agreement between themselves, they accord him a particular favour. Polygamy is the heritage of Semitic nomadism and has its orgin in the fact that in warring tribes the women were always more numerous than the men, and had need of family attachment and protection. The restriction to four wives was already a sacrifice in relation to the pre-Islamic custom amongst the Arabs.

Since it is not easy to provide for several wives—which, to say the least, implies a sufficiency of means—the majority of Moroccans have only one wife. Unmarried men beyond the age of adolescence are rare and are not looked on with favour. According to a saying of the Prophet, marriage is 'half of the religion'. The community therefore uses all means to facilitate the marriage of young people, either by finding a spouse for them, or by collecting the sum of money which the bridegroom must pay to the bride's father in respect of the dowry with which he must provide his daughter.

Europeans tend to to look on Muslim polygamy as sexual licence. In so doing, they forget that the 'licence' is largely compensated for by the monastic seclusion of family life. The essential point, however, is that Islamic marriage presupposes a completely different spiritual prototype from that of Christian marriage: Christian monogamy reflects the marriage of the church—or the soul—to Christ, and this union is founded on a personal and non-transferable love. Islamic polygamy on the other hand finds its justification in the relationship of the one Truth (*al-Ḥaqq*), to its several animic 'vessels': man, as spiritual officiant (*imām*), of his family, represents the Truth; his role corresponds to the 'active' vessel, namely the Spirit, whereas his wife corresponds to the 'passive' vessel, namely the soul. This is also why a Muslim man may marry a Christian or Jewish woman, whereas a Muslim woman may only take a husband of the same faith as herself. These spiritual prototypes—in both cases—are not something imposed on marriage from the outside, but inhere in the nature of things. The symbolism in question is not necessarily in everyone's consciousness, far from it, but it is inherent in the respective tradition, and therefore part of the collective mentality.

In Christian eyes, Muḥammad is diminished because he married several wives. In Muslim eyes, on the contrary, sexual union is ennobled by the example of the Prophet, and in a sense sanctified.

The widespread view amongst Europeans that woman is looked down on in Islam is completely at odds with the profound respect that sons show to their mothers. Every man has a mother and sees in his own wife the mother of his children. The Prophet said: 'Paradise lies at the feet of mothers.'

If it is rare for the husband to see his wife before marriage, divorce is relatively easy, although the Prophet said: 'Of the things that God has allowed, there is none that He hates more than divorce.' In the case of divorce, the husband must give back to the wife everything she brought with her into the marriage, and he must provide for the children.

Apart from their encounter in marriage, men and women live—or lived, since the way of life is changing more and more quickly—in two separate worlds. The man avoids involving his wife in his professional activity, or even mentioning her before other men. Indeed, the golden rule is that during his work the man should not think of his wife at all, and likewise, when he is with his wife, he should leave aside all thought of professional matters. Thanks to this separateness of the lives of men and women, the specifically masculine and feminine characteristics are greatly accentuated.

The Koran forbids that a woman who wishes to remain single in order to devote herself entirely to God should be forced into marriage. On the other hand, the Islamic tradition, like St. Paul, sees in a woman's marriage, a way to her salvation. In the seventeenth century there lived in Fez a woman called Fāṭima, of whom al-Kattānī writes:

> One day, when he was on a journey, Shaykh Ibrāhīm as-Suārī of Tunis fell ill in a lonely place, and was unable to move from it. Then he saw a dove flying towards him. When it reached him, it changed into a woman, who gave him some *harīra*, a soup made with germinated wheat, and attended to all his needs. She kept coming back to him, until he had fully recovered. He asked her who she was, and she replied; 'My name is Fāṭima, daughter of so and so in Fez. When thou returnest there, ask for me in the street of the barbers, in the house of so and so; there shalt thou find me.' When later the Shaykh reached Morocco and came to Fez, in

> order to visit the master Abu'l-ᶜAbbās as-Sabtī, he enquired about this house, and made his way to it. He knocked on the door, and she came out and bade him welcome. He remained as her guest. In the evening a man arrived at the house in a drunken condition and with his clothes soiled with mud. The woman washed his feet, purified his garments, prepared his bed, and did everything that a wife can do for her husband. The Shaykh stayed with them as a guest for three days. He watched the woman perform her housework and her daily prayers, and noticed that in her observance of her religious duties she did no more than the legal minimum, and adorned herself and behaved like all other women. He was greatly perplexed, and asked her how she had acquired that miraculous spiritual station which he had seen in her when he was ill. She answered him: 'Because I have accomplished, for the love of God, the duties that He has laid on me with regard to my husband.'
>
> (*Salwāt al-Anfās*)

At the time that I was living in Fez, women did not appear in the streets unless swathed in white sheets, and wearing a veil that left only their eyes visible. Only servants, and peasant women come to attend the market, showed their faces. One might have thought that women were excluded from social life but, in fact, they were very much present, hidden behind their veils, or sheltered behind curtains. Nothing happened in town without their being aware of it. To see without being seen: this was their privilege, one which they have lost with much regret, and only by having to yield to a a series of political pressures. It was thus not male tyranny that kept them prisoners of the veil, though in many other respects men were not exempt from blame. Averroes (Ibn Rushd) had in his day reproached Moroccans for neglecting the spiritual education of their daughters. In this there was a failing and a vulnerability which modern materialistic influence has exploited to the ultimate degree.

Be that as it may, the higher the social rank a woman considered herself to have, the stricter she was about veiling herself in public. The Koran merely requires that a woman should conceal her charms from men who are not blood relatives. Bedouin women, who need to be free in their movements, interpret this prescription differently than do city women, who gladly emphasize their inaccessibility. Once again city customs have led to exaggeration and narrowness, which today, under the influence of the modern world, threaten to turn into their exact opposite.

Until not so long ago, the richer families still possessed black slaves, of both sexes, who were looked upon as members of the family. Although slavery was abolished by the French, most of these Negroes remained with their former masters. Even though socially the slave was of a low rank, he was recognized, by virtue of his being a Muslim, as having the same dignity as every other believer. Historically, slavery can be explained by the law of war of nomadic and semi-nomadic peoples, for whom it was not possible to keep prisoners in camps. When the prisoners were not ransomed by their relatives, they remained the slaves of their captors until they could redeem themselves by their own work, or until their master accorded them their freedom, an act which the Koran and the *sunna* declare to be particularly pleasing to God, and which constitutes an expiatory sacrifice for a multitude of sins of omission. It was only later, with the development of city culture that the obtaining of slaves in Black Africa became an end in itself, while the struggle for the propagation of the faith served as a pretext. Since, however, the Islamic perspective does not permit the despising of any race, slavery in Islamic countries never assumed the brutal character which it had in ancient Rome and, in the nineteenth century, in the southern states of America. The slave was never considered as a mere 'object'; if he were treated unjustly, he could ask the judge to order his master to sell him. As a human being, he had a right to respect; the fact that he was not free, did not of itself contradict his humanity, since all men are the 'slaves of God'.

As the sun sets, women and girls have the habit of climbing onto the flat roofs of the houses, sometimes visiting one another by crossing over the vertiginously high walls, and sometimes merely walking along the edges of the walls, their voluminous garments caught by the evening wind. At that hour men are forbidden to go onto the roofs, and can only see the women from the distance, like flowers in the twilight. Sometimes a few young girls will clap their hands, while one of their number will improvise a dance, with short steps and swinging hips.

The Islamic house is not merely a world on its own, it is a universe transformed into a crystal; it is in this way that it is symbolically described in Oriental legends: with its four directions, the vault of heaven high above it, and the gushing fountain at its innermost centre.

From the day's first light until darkness, the sun's course can be followed, from within the courtyard of the house, along the cedar beams which form the four inside edges of the open roof. In some houses, the manner of intertwining of these beams cuts out a section of sky that looks like an octagonal eye.

The decorations on the beams catch the light and appear as combs of precious honey generously dripping in the twilight. Only at midday does the sunlight fall dazzlingly onto the tiles, so that the courtyard is caught in an ardent glow. After dark, the splendor of the African night-sky, with its black depths and its silver fords, moves slowly like the movement of a clock. When morning comes, the doves descend from the roofs. From this private world, the town and its agitation are entirely shut out. At most, one may hear, in the distance, the beat of a drum; and five times a day, the call of the muezzin resounds through the air. On the one hand, the house is closed in on itself; on the other, it is ever open to the Infinite.

6 Traditional Science

In Moorish Spain traditional science had reached such a peak that its influence was felt not only in the Maghrib, but also throughout Latin Christendom. Christian scholars in their writings explicitly referred to their Arab predecessors, and the Benedictine monk Adelhard of Bath, at the beginning of the twelfth century, wrote as follows:

> Lest it be thought that one as ignorant as I have fashioned these thoughts for myself, I do declare that they derive from my studies of the Arabs. I do not wish—should anything I say displease certain limited minds—to be the one who displeases them, for I know full well what the truly wise must expect from the common run of men. Therefore I take care not to speak for myself; I speak only for the Arabs. (*Adelhard of Bath*)

By the time the Christian kings reconquered Toledo, and later Córdoba, the highpoint of Moorish culture had already been passed. Nevertheless, the booty, in the form of books, which they appropriated, decisively influenced the formation of the medieval Schools. No less was the treasure that was taken to the already existing centres of culture in North Africa by the Moors who sought refuge there. Neverthess, in the view of Ibn Khaldūn, who himself came from a family of scholars and diplomats that had fled from Seville to the Maghrib, and who was called by the Merinids from Tunis to Fez, the treasury of knowledge that was saved was small in comparison with what was lost:

> The principal centres of sedentary culture in the (Islamic) west were Kairuan in the Maghrib and Córdoba in Spain. When these two centres

> declined, the teaching of the sciences came to a halt. A portion of it remained alive in Marrakesh under the Almohads. But because of the nomadic origin of the Almohads and the brevity of their rule, sedentary culture did not develop deep roots there . . . As a result, after the destruction of the scientific tradition in Córdoba and Kairuan, Fez and the other cities of the Maghrib remained without sound instruction . . .
> (*Muqaddima* 6:7)

In contradiction to this, a scholar named Abū'l Ḥasan ʿAlī ibn Maymūn, towards the end of the fifteenth century, wrote about Fez as follows:

> In my whole life, I have never seen its equal nor have I seen any other scholars who have so perfectly preserved the sacred law in word and deed (as well as the writings of its formulator, Imām Mālik), and who have so perfectly mastered the other sciences, such as jurisprudence, Koranic exegesis, and expertise in *ḥadīth* (the sayings of the Prophet). In Fez one finds masters of all branches of intellectuality, such as grammar, law of inheritance, mathematics, chronometry, geometry, metaphysics, logic, rhetoric, music, etc., and these masters know all the relevant texts by heart. Whoever does not know by heart the basic text relating to the science about which he speaks, and who cannot, on any question, quote it verbatim, will receive no attention; as a scholar, he will not be taken seriously. Since I left the city—it was in the year 901 (1495 A.D.)—I have seen nothing that can be compared with Fez and its scholars, either in the other cities of the Maghrib such as Tlemsen, Bujāya, or Tunis, or in any part of Syria or the Hejaz. (*Salwāt al-Anfās*)

The apparent contradiction between the two opinions cited is explained by the fact that the Aristotelian philosophy and natural sciences which had flourished in the old Andalusia found virtually no continuation in the Maghrib; it was Latin Christendom that was destined to inherit these. The Maghrib on the other hand appropriated to itself the Islamic sciences and, with the instinct for the essential characteristic of the North African genius, it traced this highly ramified science back to its principal divisions, finally giving pride of place to Koranic legal science (*al-fiqh*). Thus many blossoms fell from the tree of the sciences; but its branches and its trunk, which had their roots in Koranic doctrine, remained firm. In a modern world in which science has been pulverized into thousands of specialities, each subject to hypotheses and constantly changing experiments, traditional science (the medieval *scientia*) stands out like a harmonious and perfect work of art.

MULAY ʿALĪ

People had spoken to me of Mulay ʿAlī as one who possessed both 'outward' and 'inward' science. But no one had been willing to take me to see him, being fully aware that he shunned any contact that could give rise to public curiosity. Many regarded him as the spiritual successor of his grandfather Mulay al-ᶜArabī ad-Darqāwī who, at the beginning of the nineteenth century had revivified Islamic mysticism in its purest form and of his father, Mulay Ṭayyib, who had been the grand master of the Darqāwī spiritual order. But since the French protectorate was showing all too much interest in the fate of this order, he himself had declined any office in it, and lived as a simple scholar, teaching Arabic and law at the Koranic university of Al-Qarawiyyīn.

In the spring of 1933 I made up my mind to visit him in his house in Fez. He received me without too many questions, motioned me to sit down on a low cushion in his large bare room, took up an old Arabic book, and began to read to me about the second coming of Christ at the end of time. Since I was not sitting directly in front of him, and since he had allowed the hood of his jellaba to slip backwards from his head, I could readily observe his noble and already aged face. It expressed a two-fold nobility: his descent from the Prophet—or at any rate from the peak of Arab aristocracy—showed itself in the clear bold line of forehead and nose and in the fine contours of his temples and cheeks which were sharply illumined by light from the inner courtyard; it made me think of the most noble of the faces in El Greco's 'Burial of Count Orgaz'. But in addition his features were marked by a spiritual discipline—the consciously assumed inheritance of his illustrious forefathers—which emphasized their simplicity and sobriety.

As I was marvelling at the human frame, the culmination of so much venerable tradition, I had not yet fully awakened to his intellectual alertness, which every now and again would suddenly focus on me in a detached but searching manner, only to change back immediately into a simple goodness.

The text which he read aloud to me and on which he occasionally made brief comments in Moroccan dialect, was a collection of prophecies, partly symbolic and partly literal, which the Prophet and certain of his immediate successors had made with regard to the forthcoming end of the world. Mulay ᶜAlī had undoubtedly chosen this text in order to show me what Christ meant for him. In fact, he spoke of his second coming as if it were immediately imminent, and at one moment he pointed to himself and said: 'If our Lord ᶜIsā (Jesus) should return to earth before I die, I would immediately rise and follow him!'

Belief in Christ's second coming is firmly rooted in Islamic tradition: he will return to earth before the end of time to judge men 'with the sword of Muḥammad', to kill the antichrist (*ad-dajjāl*), and to lead the elect into a new and better world arising out of the destruction of the old one. Only true believers will be able to withstand Christ's gaze; unbelievers will perish under it. But before Christ comes, the antichrist will appear in order to lead men astray by his false promises and seeming wonders. He will call evil good, and good evil. A stream of water and a stream of fire will accompany him; whoever

FAR RIGHT, ABOVE: *Courtyard of the Qarawiyyīn from above.*

FAR RIGHT, BELOW: *Praying in the Qarawiyyīn mosque.*

should drink the water will taste fire, and whoever should touch the fire, will feel cool water. According to a saying of the Prophet, the antichrist is not simply one man. A whole series of false prophets will arise, which means that one can never be sure which of the various signs prophesied apply to one or the other of them. Only those who live through these events will know exactly what, in these prophecies, is to be taken literally or symbolically.

Before the end of the world takes place, and before the antichrist as such appears, the 'rightly-guided one' or *mahdī*, a descendant of Muḥammad, will come to gather together the faithful and lead them into battle against the powers of darkness. When before battle, the believers are gathered together for prayer 'beside the white minaret of Damascus', Christ will descend from the clouds. Under his reign a new and better age will begin, but this too will end when Gog and Magog, two hideous tribes, break through the wall which Alexander the Great, at God's command, had built against them, and overrun the earth. Christ, with the elect, will retreat to Mount Sinai, until, through his prayers and those of his faithful, the armies of darkness are destroyed, and a flood purifies the earth. Only then, on a rejuvenated earth, will the millennium begin, at the end of which a new degeneration will gradually set in, until the day of the Last Judgement arrives. 'But God knows best,' added Mulay ᶜAlī, 'when and how all this will happen.' Then he mentioned the signs which, according to a well-known saying of the Prophet, will herald the end of the present age: 'the maid-servant will give birth to her mistress, and bare-footed shepherds will vie with one another in building tall buildings.' These things, he said, were already happening, for the words about the maid-servant giving birth to her mistress was a reference to the destruction of the natural social order, and the construction of high buildings 'by poor shepherds' was already taking place. The Sufis (the Islamic mystics) interpreted these sayings in yet another, and more inward, sense; but the one interpretation does not exclude the other. All of a sudden Mulay ᶜAlī looked me straight in the face, surprising me by the severity of his regard, and said emphatically, 'The antichrist is already born.'

Such was my first meeting with this venerable elder who, contrary to my expectation, declared himself ready to teach me the fundaments of traditional Arab science (*scientia*).

THE QARAWIYYĪN UNIVERSITY

Every morning Mulay ᶜAlī would walk down from the high-lying district in which he lived to the Qarawiyyīn university, carefully gathering up his immaculately white garments as he made his way through the tumult of beasts of burden trotting uphill covered with sweat, and the swarms of porters imperiously demanding right of way. Over his jellaba and turban he wore a wide burnous, but without anything that might indicate his rank. And yet it often happened that some peasant from out of town, who was bringing his wares to the market, would timidly approach him in order to kiss his hand or

the hem of his garment. At midday he made the return journey uphill on a mule with a red saddle which a servant held ready for him at the door of the Qarawiyyīn.

The Qarawiyyīn mosque and university consists of wide halls supported by many pillars, ranged around a lengthy courtyard where fountains sparkle in the sun. The light shines from the courtyard into the halls, pours onto the woven mats covering the floors, and reaches as far as the arches joining the many pillars. Each man of learning has the custom of sitting by one particular pillar, and, as he leans against it, his students squat on the mats, and form a semi-circle facing him. Men of the people and peasants from the countryside who visited the mosque would often sit down, at a respectful distance from him, in order to hear something of the sacred science. Instruction was in the form of a conversation; one of the students would read from a classical work, and the teacher would occasionally interrupt him, in order to give explanations. Sometimes students would put questions or make objections, to which the master would reply. Sometimes this didactic conversation would become rapid and lively like an altercation. In this it would resemble what in the Middle Ages was called a *disputatio*. Nevertheless Mulay ᶜAlī was against any overdue haste. He did not permit an author to be referred to hastily or without the student wishing him God's grace, nor did he allow anyone to anticipate the proper logical development of a thought. Each brick in the edifice of a doctrine had first to be sharply cut and polished before the next one was added to it. And although the young men who listened to him may have been afflicted with an inner disquiet and secretly longed for the seductions and excitements of the modern science that had come from Europe, they nonetheless paid full attention, under his strict surveillance, to the measured and prudent teachings of their master.

When his listeners had departed, he would sometimes remain for a while facing the direction of Mecca. Then he was a picture of inwardness; his skin became as smooth and clear as wax; the contours of his cheek bones turned even sharper. As if enlarged by a hidden fire, his eyes looked into the distance. He was visibly closer to the next world than to this one. He sat upright, almost motionlessly; only a scarcely visible rapid swaying of his body seemed to suggest the invisible flowing of grace between him and Heaven.

From time to time Mulay ᶜAlī received me in a friend's orchard, in order to read Arabic texts with me. He chose these texts so that they might not only be useful to me linguistically, but would also demonstrate some aspect or other of tradition. Often, when I arrived at the orchard, which lay within the city walls encircled by high hedges of bamboo, and crossed over a narrow dyke that facilitated the irrigation of the low-lying beds of mint and melons, he would already be sitting there, under an old fig-tree, on a red mat that he always carried with him.

According to a famous saying of the Prophet, the Islamic tradition rests on three fundamental principles, namely: resignation to the Divine Will (*al-islām*), faith (*al-imān*), and spiritual virtue (*al-iḥsān*). The Divine Will makes itself known in the revealed religious law (*sharīʿa*) and in destiny. The object of faith is the doctrine of the unity and omnipotence of God, of the divine mission of all prophets—including Jesus—up to Muḥammad, and of life after death. As for spiritual virtue—or sincerity—it is by means of this that ordinary faith becomes inward certainty, and that outward conformity to the law becomes total abandonment to the will of God. Spiritual virtue was defined by the Prophet as follows: 'It is that thou shouldst worship God as if thou sawest Him; for if thou seest Him not, He nevertheless seeth thee.'

The instruction that is provided in the Koranic universities relates to the first two principles just mentioned, namely to the contents of the faith, which are enshrined in the dogmas, and to the law which, on the one hand, determines divine worship (the rites) and, on the other hand, determines the social order. The exact knowledge of the third principle, spiritual virtue, exceeds the bounds of scholastic instruction, which has been called 'the science of the outward'. It is the prerogative of the contemplative sage or mystic, the Sufi, who alone has access to 'the science of the inward'. In the Islamic world mysticism is regarded as a science, which is handed down from master to disciple just like jurisprudence, with this difference, that from the disciple a special qualification, or more exactly, an inward vocation, is required. In addition, theoretical learning must go hand in hand with spiritual practice, which alone is capable of disclosing the content of the propositions and the symbols that are taught.

THE ARABIC LANGUAGE

Most of the students at the Qarawiyyīn are preparing themselves for the profession of advocate or judge. The law is dependent upon the Koran. Since the language of the Koran has many levels of meaning and therefore cannot be perfectly translated, a knowledge of classical Arabic is the foundation of all studies. Even more, it is the key to a whole intellectual and spiritual world. According to an Arab proverb: 'Wisdom reveals herself in the dialectic of the Greeks, the craftsmanship of the Chinese, and the language of the Arabs.' In fact, classical Arabic combines a rigorously logical, almost algebraic structure, with a well-nigh unlimited capacity to form words. Almost all Arabic words can be reduced to simple tri-consonantal roots, from which, by means of reduplication, sound-shifting, and addition—all according to a system of rules—a whole tree of semantically-related verbs, nouns, and adjectives can be derived. 'The Arabic language,' said a European philologist, 'would be of an amazing intellectual transparency, if the choice of phonetic roots, from which hundreds of words derive, did not seem to be so completely arbitrary.' According to Sufi tradition, however, if the meaning of these roots is not rationally explicable, it is nevertheless intuitively intelligible.

It has recently been discovered that amongst all living Semitic languages,

ABOVE:
In the courtyard of the Qarawiyyīn.

Arabic possesses the richest and therefore the most ancient vocabulary. It is closely related to the language of Hammurabi and therefore also to the language of Abraham. That an ancient language should possess such a subtle gradation of meaning is not strange, for the younger a language is, the more its forms are simplified. What surprises scholars, however, is that a language which was first committed to writing so recently (namely in the seventh century), has preserved so much of its early inheritance. The explanation lies in the timeless manner of thinking of the nomads, and also in the fact that the nomad jealously protects and cultivates his language as his only inalienable possession. The Arabian desert also contributed to the preservation of this ancient Semitic language. And this is strong testimony to the spiritual richness of nomadism, which possesses no visible or outward sign, no image, no building, no script, and no craftmanship.

The simplest form of the Arabic word, its root form, is the verb (*verbum* – word), and therein lies a profound meaning, an indication that every phenomenon is nothing other than a happening, a manifestation developing in time, so that language transposes everything into a phonetic happening. One day Mulay ᶜAlī with an other-worldly expression on his face, looked straight at me—or rather straight through me—and said: 'All things other than God are ephemeral in themselves. I do not say that they are transient because one day they will no longer exist, I say that they are ephemeral now and always, and have never been anything other than ephemeral!'

According to Islamic tradition, it is the duty of every believer, to the limit of his intellectual capacity, to think out the contents of his faith to the end. 'Seek ye science' (*ᶜilm*), said the Prophet, 'even if it be in China.' And on another occasion he said: 'One hour of reflection is worth more than two years of religious service.' Thought, however, has an upper limit: 'Reflect on the Divine Qualities and Acts, and not on the Divine Essence.'

THEOLOGY

Islamic theology is a rational science which does not lose sight of the fact that its object, Divine Reality, cannot be grasped mentally; and this implies no contradiction: when reason recognizes its own limits, it transcends them, in a certain sense; it behaves rather like the surveyor who, from various locations, takes a sighting on a point which is inaccessible to him. This perspective makes it possible, without any illogic, on the one hand, to deny all limits, characteristics, and forms with regard to God and, on the other, to refer back to Him all the perfect aspects of existence such as beauty, goodness and power. The same also applies to apparently contradictory propositions, for example, that man possesses free choice, and that man can do nothing that God has not already foreseen and predetermined for him. That necessity and freedom are both present in God may not be graspable by the reason, but it is so by the intellect, just as is the simultaneous presence in God of past, present, and future.

The situation is similar in the case of the idea of Divine Unity (*tawḥīd*), which is the keystone of the whole doctrinal edifice. The highest meaning of unity cannot be exhausted mentally; it opens onto the Infinite; and yet one can understand unity at all levels of spiritual insight. That God is One is in principle apparent to all, and this is the basis of the unshakable cohesion of Islamic thought.

JURISPRUDENCE

Islamic jurisprudence (*fiqh*) concerns on the one hand the prescriptions with regard to divine worship—profession of faith, ritual ablution, prayer, fasting, almsgiving, pilgrimage—and on the other hand the social institutions, from questions of inheritance to the regulations for buying and selling.

The two pillars of jurisprudence are tradition and the logical principles by means of which the laws mentioned in the Koran may be applied to individual cases.

What in the Koran itself is mentioned only briefly and in a general manner, is completed by the transmission, originally oral but later written, of the sayings (*ḥadīth*) and the practice (*sunna*) of the Prophet. The testing of each individual tradition with regard to authenticity, bearing in mind the greater or lesser reliability of the transmitters, is a widely diversified science that makes great demands on the memory, requiring not only a knowledge of all the attested sayings of the Prophet—and there are thousands of them—but also of the chain of transmitters for each individual saying.

In Sunni Islam there are four classical schools of law, which differ from one another, firstly, as regards the extent to which they follow the Prophet's practice as it was maintained in Medina during the first Islamic centuries, and, secondly, as regards the extent to which they make use of decision by analogy (*ijtihād*), in order to make the proper transition from a known case to an unknown one. The people of the Maghrib belong to the legal school of Mālik ibn Anas who, more than any of the other three founders, holds fast to the practice of Medina. Since it is not possible today to find any testimonies which the founders of the four schools did not already know, any innovation can only be a deviation from the general tradition, and that is why the representatives of traditional jurisprudence defend themselves strongly against all 'reforms' proposed by Arab nationalists.

THE KORAN

For the European, whose imagination as to what a holy book is has been fashioned by the Bible or perhaps by Oriental scriptures such as the Bhagavad-Gita or the Sayings of the Buddha, the Koran is at first sight disappointing. For the Koran is neither a narrative, like the Gospels, in which the Divine appears in a humanly graspable form, nor a lucidly constructed metaphysical doctrine. Its form seems to be arbitrary, and is in fact a collection of individual revelations, providing answers to the questions and needs of the first Muslim community, and exhibiting sudden changes of content, so that one can find side by side references to Divine things and to very human things. Finally, the Biblical stories which the Koran re-tells, are presented in an unexpected, abbreviated and dry manner that seems strange to the Christian. They are deprived of their epic character and are inserted as didactic examples of an infinitely various praise of God.

It is only when one considers individual Koranic verses and begins to be aware of their many levels of meaning, that one can assess the powerful spiritual effect which this book has been able to exert, and realize why it has become the daily nourishment of thousands of contemplatively inclined people.

For the Muslim who reads the Gospel for the first time, the disappointment and surprise are scarcely less. On one occasion I brought Mulay ʿAlī, who knew Christianity only from the Islamic point of view and on the basis of those orally transmitted sayings of Christ that eventually found their way into Arabic books, a recent Arabic translation of the four Gospels. He was visibly disappointed that the Gospels, unlike the Koran, did not take the form of Divine speech, but consisted of reports on Christ's life. In the Koran, God speaks in the first person. He describes Himself and makes known His laws. The Muslim is therefore inclined to consider each individual sentence of the holy Book as a separate revelation and to experience the words themselves, and even their very sound, as a means of grace. Mulay ʿAlī was put off both by the easygoing style of the translation and by the fact that the meaning lay more in the event described than in this or that verbal formula. He looked for verses that described God's qualities, His majesty, His omnipotence, and scarcely found any. I had to explain to him that the Gospels could only be completely understood against the background of the Old Testament.

What surprised him most was that God was called 'Father' and Christ 'Son'; for between father and son, he said, there was a similarity of nature which the incomparability of God excluded. To this I remarked that the expression 'son of God' meant that Jesus had no human father, which the Koran itself teaches, and that furthermore his spirit emanated from God and was of the same essence of God, which the Koran also maintains, when it says that Christ is 'Word of God and Spirit of God'. Mulay ʿAlī answered that this meaning was indeed acceptable, even if it touched on secrets which human language was more likely to misrepresent than to express.

Through his whole education Mulay ʿAlī was too much the Islamic man of learning—centred on the doctrinal unequivocalness of his own tradition—to come to terms with the completely different speech and symbolism of a religion that was foreign to him. Therein he differed, as I was later to learn, from many other representatives of the 'science of the inward'. Thus the Sufi master Aḥmad ibn Muṣṭafā al-ʿAlāwī, who at that time lived in Mostaghanem in Algeria and had many disciples from Morocco, said to a Catholic priest: 'If you accept that expressions like 'God the Father' and 'Son of God' are symbols which can be interpreted metaphysically, then there is nothing that separates us from you.'

'Consider the lilies of the field; they toil not, neither do they spin; and yet I say unto you that even Solomon in all his glory was not arrayed like one of these.' These words of Christ have the same ring about them as the Koran, according to which everything in Heaven and earth is a 'sign' from God. In order better to understand what the Koran means for the ordinary Muslim, I once observed a group of men who, early in the morning, before the sun had risen, were chanting the Koran in unison in the courtyard of the Qarawiyyīn mosque. The Arabic language is rich in sounds, from the characteristic gutterals to every abrupt or reverberating sound that it is possible for lips and palate to produce; it is as if the whole body were speaking. When all these natural drums and cymbals accommodate themselves to the inimitable rhythm of the Koran, when this rhythm is borne by a triumphant and solemn melody, and when all of this is united with the meaning of the words, there is born that unique effect that overwhelms every Arab listener.

FAR RIGHT: *Maghribi Koran 18th century.*

When the chanters reached the verse: *'To God belong the Heavens and the*

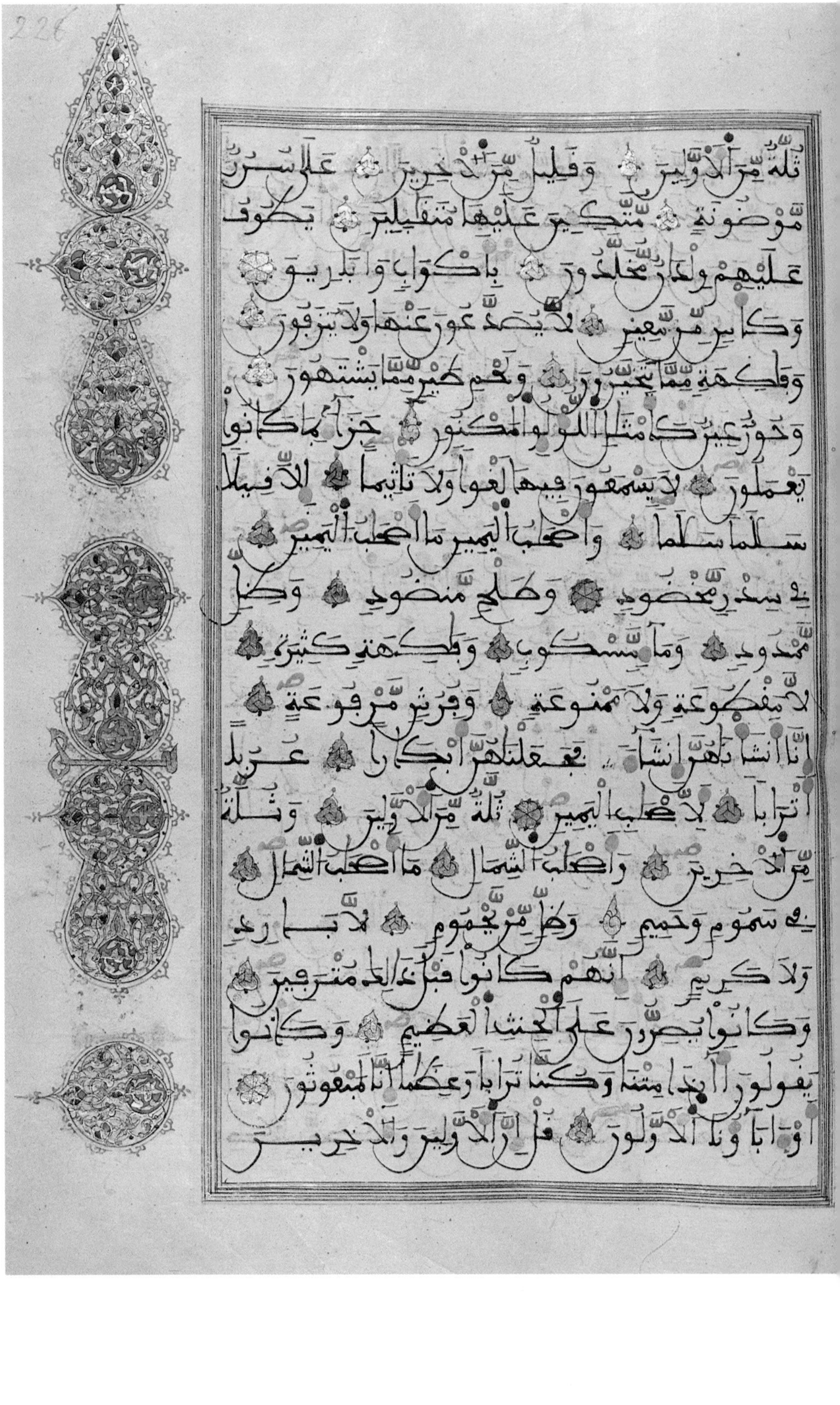
226

ثلة من الأولين وقليل من الآخرين على سرر
موضونة متكئين عليها متقابلين يطوف
عليهم ولدان مخلدون بأكواب وأباريق
وكأس من معين لا يصدعون عنها ولا ينزفون
وفاكهة مما يتخيرون ولحم طير مما يشتهون
وحور عين كأمثال اللؤلؤ المكنون جزاء بما كانوا
يعملون لا يسمعون فيها لغوا ولا تأثيما إلا قيلا
سلاما سلاما وأصحاب اليمين ما أصحاب اليمين
في سدر مخضود وطلح منضود وظل
ممدود وماء مسكوب وفاكهة كثيرة
لا مقطوعة ولا ممنوعة وفرش مرفوعة
إنا أنشأناهن إنشاء فجعلناهن أبكارا عربا
أترابا لأصحاب اليمين ثلة من الأولين وثلة
من الآخرين وأصحاب الشمال ما أصحاب الشمال
في سموم وحميم وظل من يحموم لا بارد
ولا كريم إنهم كانوا قبل ذلك مترفين
وكانوا يصرون على الحنث العظيم وكانوا
يقولون أئذا متنا وكنا ترابا وعظاما أئنا لمبعوثون
أوآباؤنا الأولون قل إن الأولين والآخرين

نضاختان ۝ فبأي ءالاء ربكما تكذبان ۝ فيهما
فاكهة ونخل ورمان ۝ فبأي ءالاء ربكما تكذبان ۝
فيهن خيرات حسان ۝ فبأي ءالاء ربكما
تكذبان ۝ حور مقصورات في الخيام ۝ فبأي
ءالاء ربكما تكذبان ۝ لم يطمثهن إنس قبلهم
ولا جان ۝ فبأي ءالاء ربكما تكذبان ۝ متكئين
على رفرف خضر وعبقري حسان ۝ فبأي ءالاء ربكما
تكذبان ۝ تبارك اسم ربك ذي الجلال والإكرام ۝

بسم الله الرحمن الرحيم
إذا وقعت الواقعة ۝ ليس لوقعتها كاذبة ۝ خافضة
رافعة ۝ إذا رجت الأرض رجا ۝ وبست الجبال
بسا ۝ فكانت هباء منبثا ۝ وكنتم أزواجا
ثلاثة ۝ فأصحاب الميمنة ۝ ما أصحاب الميمنة ۝
وأصحاب المشأمة ۝ ما أصحاب المشأمة ۝ والسابقون
السابقون ۝ أولئك المقربون ۝ في جنات النعيم ۝

earth, and to God the journey returneth. Sawest thou not how God guideth the clouds, gathereth them together, and disposeth of them?', one of the men raised his eyes to the early morning sky as if he perceived the cloud gathering; and at the following words: *'then seest thou the rain-drops fall from their midst'*, his eyes moved downwards from the heavens to the earth. The recitation continued: *'From Heaven doth He send down mountains of hail, as a visitation on whomsoever He will'*—the man looked round about him—*'and which He holdeth back from whomsoever He will. The glare of His lightning almost removeth the sight from men's eyes'*—the man looked as if he had been blinded. Finally his face showed repose at the words: *'God suffereth the night to follow the day; verily therein dwelleth a sign for those who see.'*

THE MYSTIC

Mulay ᶜAlī was of the view that in our age only very few people were capable of understanding Sufi wisdom, and that it was better to remain silent about it than to speak. If he were asked about the inward states that Sufis attain, he would decline to answer, saying: 'These are fruits that grow for themselves on the tree of divine service; let us rather speak of how to care for the tree and how to water it, and not of its fruits, before they are ripe.' And to a young man who had asked him to accept him as his disciple on the way of contemplation, he replied: 'Dear friend, the relationship between spiritual master and spiritual disciple is something so elevated that we would be very daring if we sought to establish it. Let us rather speak of the things we should be doing.' And he gave him the advice that he felt was right for him. His reticence was perhaps also caused by the *wahhābī* influences, hostile to mysticism, which at that time had gained a certain foothold amongst the students. Nevertheless, he decided on one occasion to make Al-Ghazālī's famous work *The Revivification of the Religious Sciences* the subject of his lectures. This work was recognized by almost all the representatives of the 'science of the outward', since the exoteric legitimacy of its standpoint is unassailable. At the same time, however, it contains several chapters which constitute a bridge from exoterism to esoterism or mysticism. At the end of his first lecture the students began to question Mulay ᶜAlī about Sufism, and one of them said: 'We can readily believe that centuries ago there were great mystics who received authentic inspirations and even possessed wonderful powers; but today all those who claim to represent Sufism are nothing but charlatans. In our day and age there are no longer any Sufis.' Mulay ᶜAlī turned to him and said, with a mildness that brooked no contradiction: 'My son, how can you set a limit to the omnipotence of God?'

Islamic mysticism was not always banned from the Qarawiyyīn university. As recently as the beginning of the century, Sufi treatises were the subject of lectures, and one of the most important representatives of mysticism in the Maghrib, the Sufi Abū ᶜAbdallāh Ibn ᶜAbbād ar-Rundī, who was born in Ronda in Andalusia in 1331, was preacher and *imām* there. A contemporary writes of him:

PREVIOUS PAGES: *Maghribi Koran, Suras 55:66–56:49.*

In Fez I met the saintly scholar Abū ᶜAbdallāh Muḥammad ibn Ibrāhīm ar-Rundī, whose father before him had been a famous preacher. The son Abū ᶜAbdallāh is distinguished by his composure, his asceticism, and his righteousness. He is the author of the verse: 'He attains no nobility who has not first weighed the clay of this earth with eternity.' I met him on the Prophet's birthday in the sultan's palace, where he had been invited to hear the spiritual singing. He manifestly did not welcome this. I have never at any other time seen him at any gathering, and whoever might wish to speak with him was obliged to see him alone. Once I requested him to pray for me. He blushed and was embarrassed, but agreed nevertheless. The only luxury he permitted himself was perfumed oils and incense. He did his own housework. He was unmarried and had no servant. At home he wore a patchwork garment, but when he went out he covered it with a green or a white robe. His disciples were all from the best and most gifted of the community . . . Today he is *imām* and preacher in the Qarawiyyīn mosque at Fez.

Al-Kattānī wrote of him: 'He had something about him that won the hearts of children. They swarmed around him, as soon as they saw him, in order to kiss his hand. But kings too sought to gain his friendship . . .

'He studied in Ronda, Fez and Tlemsen and in Salé he was the disciple of the Andalusian master Aḥmad Ibn ᶜĀshir. From there he travelled to Tangier where he met the Sufi Abū Marwān ᶜAbd al-Mālik, who was perhaps the 'unlettered man' of whom Ibn ᶜAbbād said that he alone had been able to open his inward eye . . .'

The Shaykh Abū Masᶜūd al-Harrās recalls: 'I was reciting the Koran aloud in the courtyard of the Qarawiyyīn mosque as the muezzins were making the call for the night-prayer. Suddenly I saw Ibn ᶜAbbād, in a sitting position, fly over the door of his house, across the courtyard of the mosque, and disappear into the hall that surrounds the atrium. I went to have a look, and I found him praying close to the *mihrab*.'

It is related that, as he approached death, he laid his head on the lap of one of his disciples, and began to recite the Throne Verse from the Koran. When he reached the words 'the Living, the Eternal', he continued repeating 'O God! O Living! O Eternal!' Thereupon one of those present addressed him by name and recited the continuation of the verse; but he went on with his invocation. Shortly before he passed on he was heard reciting the verse: 'The friends are leaving me, but they will return when I leave them.'

Before his death he bequeathed a sum of money which he had buried at the head of his bed. He directed that with it a piece of land should be bought, the revenue from which was to be used for the upkeep of the Qarawiyyīn mosque. When the sum of money was counted—it came to eight hundred and ten gold *mithqāl*—it was discovered that it was the

> exact amount that he had received in salary during his twenty-five years as *imām* and preacher. (*Salwāt al-Anfās*)

Ibn ᶜAbbād of Ronda left behind him several treatises on mysticism, amongst then a commentary, still much read today, on the 'Aphorisms' (*ḥikam*) of the Sufi Ibn ᶜAṭā'illah of Alexandria.

THE QARAWIYYĪN BUILDING

The building of the university and mosque of Al-Qarawiyyīn is almost as old as the city of Fez itself. In its original, considerably smaller, form, it was founded in 859 by a pious woman called Fāṭima, the daughter of a rich merchant who had migrated to Fez from Kairuan in Tunisia. About a hundred years later it was enlarged by the Berber prince Yaᶜlā of the Zenātā tribe, a vassal of ᶜAbd ar-Raḥmān III, who had the sword of Idrīs II embedded at the top of its minaret. But it was only under the Almoravids that the building reached its present proportions, with its ten transepts, each with twenty columns, and with the large halls around the courtyard. The central nave that leads up to the *mihrāb* (prayer-niche) is surmounted by five domes which are visible only from the inside. Thirteen doors open onto the surrounding streets. The two fountains, the roofs of which stand out like baldachins at each end of the courtyard, were erected during the reign of the Saadians and show the influence of the art of Granada.

Plan of the Qarawiyyīn Mosque. In the foreground is the courtyard with a fountain complex on each of its shorter sides and the minaret of the mosque on the right. The central nave of the great hall leads to the prayer-niche. A subsidiary nave leads to an annex containing the library and the mosque used for funerals.

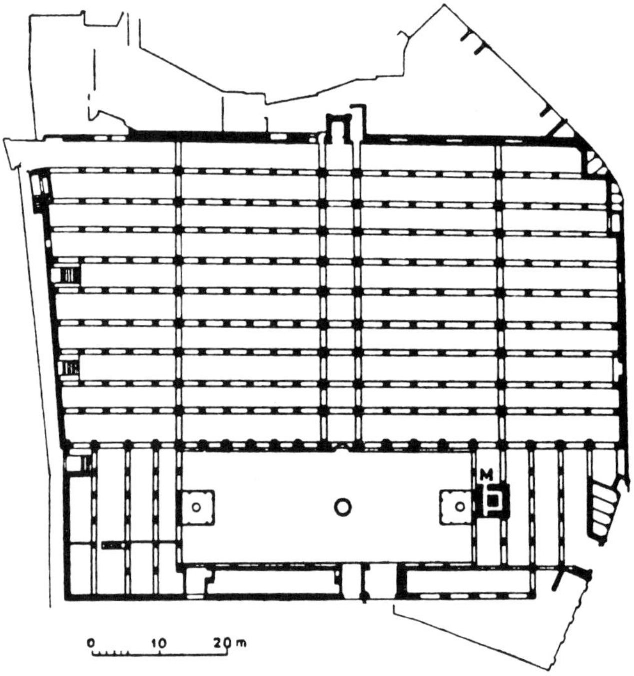

THE KEEPER OF THE TIME

At the end of the courtyard of the Qarawiyyīn rises the minaret, halfway up which there is a small room for the *muwaqqit*, the 'keeper of the time'. It is his responsibility, following the revolution of the heavens, to determine the hour and the minute at which the muezzin must announce the beginning of each of the five daily prayers. The muezzins of all the other mosques in Fez take their lead from the muezzin of Al-Qarawiyyīn.

I have forgotten the name of the *muwaqqit* who, at the time of my first visit to Morocco—that is to say between the two world wars—held this office. I have never seen a more strikingly beautiful man. He was already old, certainly over eighty, but seemed taller than everyone else, possibly because of his royal countenance, in which his widely-set light grey eyes shone, like two stars, with a victorious inward joy. His white beard fell down over his broad chest. I felt that the Patriarch Abraham must have looked like this.

In the *muwaqqit's* room in the minaret, several medieval sextants hang beside a tall pendulum-clock, which was the gift of Louis XIV to the Sultan Mulay Ismāʿīl. The finely chiselled circles and curves of the ancient instruments are reminiscent of the orbits of the heavenly bodies, whereas the complacently ostentatious baroque time-piece merely recalls the historical moment when, in a general manner, men began to measure time, not from the movement of the heavens, but according to a mechanical process. For the *muwaqqit* of the Qarawiyyīn, the movement of the heavens was still the valid

Maghribi astrolabe c.16th century.

measure. Depending on the season, the revolving of the heavens is either faster or slower than the working of a clock, and this means that a clock does not keep exactly in step with the most primordial and comprehensive measure of time—time itself being ungraspable, since the movement of the heavens resembles a rhythm more than a mechanical ticking.

The timetable for the five daily prayers, which by their rhythmical repetition reflect the timeless within time, varies according to longitude, so that a given muezzin's call is made more or less as soon as the muezzin in the locality immediately to the east of him has finished making his. In this way the proclamation of God's Oneness courses across the whole Muslim world, while the bows and prostrations of the faithful, directed towards Mecca from wherever the worshippers may be, spread through the Muslim community like a wave.

THE MONTH OF FASTING

The keeper of the time, *muwaqqit*, must also determine the beginning of each month, which begins with the appearance of the new crescent moon, and especially the beginning of the month of fasting, Ramaḍān. Since the Arab year is a lunar year and since twelve lunar months are approximately ten days shorter than a solar year, the month of fasting falls ten days earlier each solar year and thus, with time, passes through every season. When it occurs in the middle of summer, it is particularly exacting since, from the first sign of dawn until sunset, the believer who is in good health may neither eat nor drink. He must also abstain from sexual relations.

On the evening that Ramaḍān begins, the keeper of the time is not the only one on the look-out. On every roof-top people watch impatiently to see whether, following sunset, the young crescent moon will become visible. First one or two, then a quickly increasing number, espy the fine silver horn on the still light horizon. A cry of joy breaks out, for it was in this month that the Koran was revealed to the Prophet. This joy can be felt throughout the city, and it is rather similar to Christmas Eve in Christian countries.

During the final nights of Ramaḍān people keep vigil, for in one of these nights—precisely which one no one knows—the angels are said to come down from Heaven, just as they did in the Night of Revelation (or Night of Power), regarding which it is said in the Koran:

Behold, We sent it down in the Night of Power,
And what shall teach thee what is the Night of Power?
The Night of Power is better than a thousand months.
In it the angels and the Spirit descend,
By the leave of their Lord, with every decree.
Peace it is, till the rising of dawn.

In these final nights, the mosques are filled with adults and children. Many pray together, others pray on their own, and yet others recite the Koran. Then

Pool in the courtyard of the Andalūs mosque.

Worshippers making ritual ablutions in the inner courtyard of the Mosque of Mulay Idrīs II.

all the lights under the dome of the Qarawiyyīn mosque are lit and in the main nave the immense chandelier, dating from the time of the Almohads, burns brightly. Its enormous tiara of oil-lamps is strongly suggestive of the ancient symbol of the world-tree, decorated with suns and stars.

It is the same symbolism as lies behind the Christmas tree. Whether or not the craftsman who made this chandelier was conscious of the symbolism, I cannot say; but another Moroccan craftsman said to me that the universe with all its visible and invisible degrees of existence resembled a tree, whose trunk represents the one Spirit (*ar-Rūḥ*) and whose root is pure Being.

A long time ago, when this chandelier burned for the first time in celebration of the holy month of Ramaḍān, a few scholars from the town sat underneath it in the twenty-seventh night of the fast, and one of them, Abū'l-Qāṣim al-Maziātī, composed the following impromptu:

> Behold the chandelier, see how its light
> Scintillatingly rends the veil of night.

His companion Ibn ᶜAbdūn answered him in the following verses:

> Its form resembles a hill,
> On which light gathers in layers.

A third man, Mālik ibn al-Marhal, continued:

> May the Lord of the worlds protect it
> From malignant power and the evil eye.

A fourth, Muḥammad ibn Khalaf, added:

> Beauty of Islam! It shines out,
> Even as these chalices sparkle in the falling night.

A fifth, and unknown poet of that same time said of the chandelier:

> It resembles the constellation of the Pleiades.
> A wisp of air bends its flames
> And makes them quiver, like believing hearts,
> Full of awe, in the bosom of the night. (*Rawḍ al-Qirṭās*)

7 The Golden Chain

THE SPIRITUAL HIGH POINTS of Maghribi culture are to be found in the realm of Islamic mysticism, which in Arabic is known as *at-taṣawwuf*. Possessing as it does the dual aspects of wisdom and the love of God, it finds expression not only in metaphysical doctrines, but also in poetry and the visual arts, and, as its essence is communicated most directly in symbols and parables, it can speak without hindrance not only to learned believers, but also to the simple man of the people: the craftsman and the Bedouin; in fact, it may often be more readily accessible to the unlearned than to the learned. MYSTICISM

Though Islamic mysticism, as it persists in Morocco down to the present day, may be compared in many respects with Christian mysticism—and in other respects with Hindu and Far-Eastern mysticism—it is nevertheless founded entirely on the religious form specific to Islam. Its point of departure is *Tawḥīd*, the doctrine of Divine Unity. If Islamic law demands, as the first duty of every believer, that he 'testify' to the unity of God, Islamic mysticism requires that this attestation (*shahāda*), should not be merely with the lips, nor even merely with the mind, but that, beyond all reflections and sentiments, it should be a total and immediate act of testimony or witness (*shahāda*); this means nothing other than the Knowledge of God.

God can only be known, however, when the human ego, which instinctively regards itself as a self-sufficient centre—a kind of 'divinity' in addition to the Divinity—is extinguished before the infinitude of God, in accordance with the words: '*There is no divinity but God.*' This does not mean that the immortal essence of the soul has to be annihilated; what must be dissolved is the web-like substance of the soul, made up of egoistic passions and imaginings, which restrict consciousness to the level of ephemeral appearances. When this 'veil' of selfishness is lifted from the underlying Spirit or Intellect—the supra-individual faculty of direct knowledge—things are seen as they really are. God is seen in His all-embracing Presence and the creature as pure possibility contained within the Divine Being. 'The Sufi,' said the medieval spiritual master Abū'l-Ḥasan ash-Shādhilī, 'sees his own existence as particles of dust made visible by a ray of sunlight: neither real nor unreal.'

Of this same spiritual vision the famous saint Abū Madyan says in a poem:

> Everything outside of God is unreal, everything taken individually or
> collectively, when thou truly knowest it.
> Know: without Him the whole creation, including thee, would
> disappear, and come to naught.
> Whatever does not have its roots in His Being, can in no wise be real.
> The knowers of God are as if extinguished. What else can they look upon,
> but Him, the Transcendent, the Glorious?
> Everything they see outside of Him, has truly been destined for
> destruction, in the past, in the future, and in the present moment.
>
> (*al-Madanī*)

I once asked Mulay ʿAlī ad-Darqāwī about the state of the mystic who had realized this degree of contemplation. 'It is an uncovering of the Divine Unity,' he answered, 'but the servant (creature) remains a servant, and no deception can arise.'

The organ by means of which man can take cognizance of the presence of God is, according to Sufi teaching, not the brain but the heart. As with the Church fathers, the heart is seen not as the seat of the sentiments but as the seat of the Intellect or Spirit (*ar-rūḥ*), which is independent of mental forms and capable of direct knowledge.

Deflected from its true centre, which has its roots in the Eternal, the consciousness of the average man is as if imprisoned in a kind of dream or state of forgetfulness (*ghafla*). This is why man must be 'reminded' (of That which he has 'forgotten'), and this is the reason for what is known as *dhikr*, which the Sufi must practise in a large variety of ways, and which may be translated as 'remembrance', 'mention', or 'invocation'. *Dhikr* is closely related to the 'prayer of the heart' of the Hesychasts of Eastern Christianity.

Since the goal of the mystical path is the transcending of the ego, it cannot be embarked upon without grace (*tawfīq*); nor can it be followed without the help of a spiritual master (*shaykh* or *murshid*), who has himself traversed it, and without the spiritual influence or benediction which he confers on the disciple.

Islamic mysticism therefore rests on an unbroken spiritual succession or tradition which goes back, from master to master, to its origin in the Prophet Muḥammad. This esoteric tradition runs in parallel to the exoteric or law-giving tradition destined for the collectivity as a whole. At its origins are to be found those counsels given by the Prophet to only some of his companions; for the mystical way presupposes extraordinary gifts and also a vocation, which are not given to everyone.

THE SPIRITUAL SUCCESSION

This spiritual succession or tradition is often represented as a tree, whose roots are in revelation and whose twigs, leaves, and flowers correspond to the spiritual methods or 'paths' (*ṭuruq*), founded by the great spiritual master. The branches of the tree represent the principal lines of succession, and are sometimes to be interpreted historically, sometimes only symbolically. On the root of the tree one can read the name *Allāh*; above it, on the trunk, is the name of the Archangel Gabriel (Jibrīl), who, in the Islamic perspective is the divine instrument of revelation, and above this is the name of Muḥammad. At that point the trunk divides into two branches, which bear the names respectively of the first and fourth caliphs (Abū Bakr and ᶜAlī), since they were the first two mediators and masters of the Sufi tradition. These two branches divide into many twigs, which bear the names of the earliest Sufis such as Ḥasan al-Baṣrī, Ḥabīb al-ᶜAjamī and Sarī as-Saqatī. Following these come the names of the greatest spiritual masters of the first Islamic centuries such as Junayd, the great teacher of Sufi metaphysics, Dhū'n-Nūn al-Miṣrī, the lover, and Abū Yazīd al-Bistāmī, the absorbed in God. All of these masters lived in the Islamic east, although Sufi mysticism appeared as the 'inner dimension' of Islam wherever Islam prevailed. From about the fourth Islamic century onwards (the ninth century A.D.), the blossoms of mysticism also appeared in the Far West, firstly in Spain and immediately thereafter in the Maghrib, where the name Abū Madyan stands at the origin of a whole segment of new twigs and leaves. This name appears at the top of the tree at about the same level as other famous names from which henceforth almost all subsequent spiritual orders spring. For it was at that time—the twelfth century A.D.—that there appeared ᶜAbd al-Qādir al-Jīlānī in the Near East (his influence was to sweep across the whole Islamic world); Muᶜīn ad-dīn Chishtī in North India and, a little later, Jalāl ad-dīn Rūmī in Asia Minor. From this time onwards the Sufi tradition became organized in the form of spiritual orders or brotherhoods that took the name of their founders.

ABŪ MADYAN

Abū Madyan Shuᶜayb was born in Seville of Arab parents in 1126. He was orphaned at a tender age, and was apprenticed to learn the weaver's craft. He fled from his brother's house, however, with a view to quenching his thirst for knowledge. After much wandering, he finally reached Fez, where he took instruction from several of the masters of 'outward' and 'inward' science, while he made a living from weaving.

It was at this time that the works of al-Ghazālī reached Fez. The scholar

Abū'l-Ḥasan ibn Harzihim (Harazem in Moroccan dialect) condemned them publicly. During the following night he dreamt that the author had complained about him to the Prophet and the first four Caliphs and that he had been sentenced to so many blows with a whip. He awoke and found whip-marks on his body. He withdrew his condemnation and immersed himself in the writings he had proscribed. Thanks to Ibn Harzihim, Abū Madyan became acquainted not only with al-Ghazālī's *Revivification of the Religious Sciences*, but also with the works of al-Muḥāsibī and other Sufi masters.

Abū Madyan's beginnings on the spiritual path carry the seal of a vocation that is as inimitable as the beauty of virgin nature.

> At the beginning of my spiritual journey, (Abū Madyan himself relates), I attended the lectures of several spiritual masters. When I heard the explanation of a Koranic verse or a saying of the Prophet, I used to immerse myself in it completely. I would flee to an uninhabited place (on Mount Zalāgh) and apply myself to the exercises to which God had inspired me following my absorption in what I had heard. While I thus passed my time in solitude, a gazelle came to me and made friends with me. And when I encountered dogs in an out-lying village that belonged to Fez, they would crowd around me wagging their tails. One day, however, I met in Fez a man that I had known in Andalusia and he greeted me warmly. I felt that I owed him hospitality and went to get a piece of cloth in which I had wrapped eight dirhams. I looked for the man in order to give him the money, but I could no longer find him and so I took the bundle with me to the lonely place to which it was my custom to withdraw. As I walked past the village the dogs refused to come near me, and indeed prevented my passage through the village until someone came and called them off. When I reached my place of refuge, the gazelle ran past as usual, but when it scented me, it fled and seemed no longer to know me. I understood that it was all because of the money I was carrying, and I threw it away from me. The gazelle immediately became calm and was friendly with me as before. When I returned to Fez I took the money with me, and gave it to the Andalusian as soon as I saw him. Then I again went past the village, on the way to my refuge, and the dogs ran up to me wagging their tails as before. Finally the gazelle appeared again, smelt my scent from head to foot, and nestled against me. And thus I lived for a certain time.
>
> Later I heard about the spiritual master Abū Yaᶜzā (an unlettered Berber who lived in the Middle Atlas) and his miracles, about which the people were speaking. My heart was filled with love for him and I joined a party of *fuqarā'* (poor in spirit, i.e. those following a spiritual path), who were setting out on a journey in order to visit him. When we arrived at his place, he greeted everyone except me, and when a meal was brought, he

> excluded me from it. Three days did I remain thus, tormented by hunger and assailed by doubts. Then I said to myself: when the master rises up, I will rub my face on the spot where he was sitting. As soon as he stood up, I rubbed my face on the ground. When I raised myself up, I found that I was blind. Thus I remained, and I wept all night long. In the early morning the master called my name and came to me. 'O my Lord', I said to him, 'I have become blind and can no longer see!' He stroked my eyes with his hand and my sight immediately returned. Then he stroked my breast, and all doubts departed from me. At the same time my pangs of hunger vanished, and I perceived many wonders that his blessing had worked within me.
>
> Later on I begged his leave to depart from him in order to fulfil the requirements of the pilgrimage. This he granted me, and said: 'On thy way thou wilt meet a lion, pay no heed to it. If, however, fear overcome thee, say to it: "For the sake of the holiness of the men of light, depart from me!"'—And thus it came to pass . . . (*Ḥamidū*)

Having returned from the east, Abū Madyan settled in Bujāya (Bougie) and soon became the centre of a vast group of disciples. He was the living model of spiritual poverty (*faqr*), the meaning of which is expressed in the Koranic verse: *'O men, ye are the poor* (fuqarā') *in relation to God, and God is the Rich, to whom all praises are due.'* The expression *faqīr* (plural *fuqarā'*), which corresponds to the Persian expression *dervīsh*, became the term that was applied to those who followed the Sufi path. The following few words of Abū Madyan characterize his spiritual attitude:

> Trust in God until the remembrance of Him (*dhikr*) hath completely overpowered thee; for creatures are of no use to thee . . . Every spiritual truth (*ḥaqīqa*) that extinguisheth not the traces of the creature, is no (real) truth . . . Spiritual poverty is a pointer to the Divine Unity and a proof of detachment (*tafrīd*) from multiplicity. The meaning of poverty is simply this: that thou takest cognizance of nothing but Him.

When Abū Madyan was already old, the Almohad caliph Yaᶜqūb al-Manṣūr commanded him to appear at court. He feared the growing influence of the saint, or perhaps simply wished to make use of him. Abū Madyan set out on the journey, but died at ᶜUbbād, near Tlemsen, not far from the Moroccan border. It was the year 1198. His grave, over which a mosque was built, has remained a leading place of pilgrimage. The Merinid sultans of Fez enhanced it with magnificent buildings.

Two of Abū Madyan's indirect disciples were to have a lasting influence throughout the spiritual world of Islam. The first was the Arab Muhyi'd-dīn ibn ᶜArabī, who was born in 1165 in Murcia in Spain and migrated via Fez,

Bujāya, and Tunis to the Islamic east. Because of his unsurpassed metaphysical expositions he was called 'the greatest master' (*ash-Shaykh al-akbar*). The other was Abū'l-Ḥasan ash-Shādhilī, the founder of the spiritual order (*ṭarīqa*) bearing his name.

IBN ᶜARABĪ

Muḥyi'd-dīn ibn ᶜArabī grew up in Seville, when Abū Madyan, as an old man, still lived in Bujāya. Ibn ᶜArabī wrote as follows:

> Our master and imām Abū Yaᶜqūb ben Yakhlaf al-Qūmī al-ᶜAbbāsī —may God be pleased with him—had been a companion of Abū Madyan and had met several of the men of God in his country. He lived for a time in Egypt and married in Alexandria . . . He was offered the governorship of Fez, but declined it. He possessed such a sure knowledge of the spiritual way that Abū Madyan who was the founder and expounder of this way in the Maghrib, said of him: 'Abū Yaᶜqūb is like a safe harbour for a ship.' He was generous, much given to *dhikr* (remembrance of God), and gave alms in secret. He honoured the poor and humbled the rich.
>
> I was obedient to him and was educated by him—and what an education it was! . . . He had a powerful spiritual will and for the most part followed the way of the *malāmatiyya* (those who intentionally attract people's blame). Seldom was he seen without an expression of total concentration on his face. But whenever he saw a poor man, his face would light up with joy . . .
>
> Whenever I sat before him, or before any other spiritual master, I would tremble like a leaf in the wind, my voice would desert me, and I would be unable to move my limbs. People would notice this. And if the master were indulgent to me, and sought to put me at my ease, it only increased my awe and reverence for him. This master had love for me, but concealed it by showing favour to others, and by displaying a distant manner towards me, commending what others had to say while taking me to task. He went so far in this, that my companions who studied with me under his charge, began to think little of my spiritual gifts. And yet I alone of the whole group, as the master later said, reached the goal.
>
> Of my many experiences with Abū Yaᶜqūb, the following is worthy of mention. I must first explain that at the time concerned I did not yet know the *Epistle* of al-Qushayrī (a fundamental work of Islamic mysticism). I was unaware that anyone had written about this spiritual way, and did not even know what the expression *taṣawwuf* (mysticism) meant.
>
> One day the master mounted his horse, and bade me and one of my companions follow him to Muntabār, a mountain that was about an hour's ride from Seville. As soon as the city gate was opened, my companion and I set out on foot. My companion carried in his hand a copy of Al-Qushayrī's *Epistle*, of which as I have said, I knew nothing. We climbed the mountain and at the top we found our master, who, with a

servant, had gone ahead of us. He tethered his horse, and we entered a mosque at the top of the mountain in order to pray. After the prayer, we sat with our backs towards the prayer-niche (*miḥrāb*). The master handed me Qushayrī's *Epistle* and told me to read from it. I was unable, however, to utter a single word. My awe of him was so great that the book even fell from my hands. Then he told my companion to read it, and he expounded on what was read until it was time for the afternoon prayer, which we said. Then the master said: 'Let us now return to town.' He mounted his horse, and I ran alongside him, holding on to his stirrup. Along the way he talked to me of the virtues and miracles of Abū Madyan. I was all ears, and forgot myself entirely, keeping my eyes fixed on his face the whole time. Suddenly he looked at me and smiled and, spurring his horse, made me run even more quickly in order to keep up with him. I succeeded in doing so. Finally he stopped, and said to me: 'Look and see what thou hast left behind thee.' I looked back and saw that the way along which we had come was full of thorn bushes that reached as high as my tunic, and that the ground was also covered with thorns. He said: 'Look at thy feet!' I looked at them and saw on them no trace of the thorns. 'Look at thy garments!' On them too I found no trace. Then he said: 'That comes from the grace engendered by our talking about Abū Madyan—may God be pleased with him—so persevere, my son, on the spiritual path!' Thereupon he spurred his horse and left me behind . . .

(*Rūḥ al-Quds*)

ASH-SHĀDHILĪ

At the beginning of the thirteenth century of the Christian era, about twenty years after Muḥyi'd-dīn Ibn ᶜArabī had left Fez for the east, the Moroccan Abū'l-Ḥasan ᶜAlī ibn ᶜAbdallāh, a scion of the Ḥasanid branch of the Fatimids, who later achieved fame under the name of Abū'l-Ḥasan ash-Shādhilī, also migrated to the east in order to seek the spiritual pole of his time. In Baghdad a Sufi informed him that this pole was to be found in his own homeland, on Mount al-ᶜAlam in the Rif mountains. He therefore returned home, and found in the place described a disciple of Abū Madyan, namely the spiritual master ᶜAbd as-Salām ibn Mashīsh:

IBN MASHĪSH

As I approached his place of refuge, which was a cave near the top of the mountain, I made a halt at a spring which gushed forth a little beneath it. I washed myself with the intention of casting off all my previous knowledge and actions, then, as one completely poor, I made my way up to the cave. He came out towards me, and when he saw me, he said: 'Welcome, ᶜAlī, son of ᶜAbdallāh, son of ᶜAbd al-Jabbār . . .' and he named all my ancestors right back to the Prophet, whom God bless and greet. Then he said: 'O, ᶜAlī, thou comest up to me here as one poor in knowing and doing to seek from me the riches of this world and the next.' I was smitten

with fear out of awe for him. Then I remained with him for a number of days, until God opened my inward eye and I beheld wonders and things that far exceeded the ordinary realm, and I experienced the goodness of God's grace . . . One day, as I sat by my master, I said inwardly to myself: 'Who knows, perhaps my master knows the Supreme Name of God.' At that moment the young son of the master spoke from the depths of the cave: 'O Abū'l-Ḥasan, it is not a question of knowing the Supreme Name of God, it is a question of being the Supreme Name.' Thereupon the Shaykh said: 'My young son has seen through thee and recognized thee!'
(*al-Madanī*)

Tomb of Mulay ᶜAbd as-Salām ibn Mashīsh.

ᶜAbd as-Salām ibn Mashīsh was murdered in 1228. His tomb on Mount al-ᶜAlam, is a place of pilgrimage to this day.

Only one text has come down to us from Ibn Mashīsh, a metaphysical paraphrase of a widely known prayer, in which the believer calls on God to bless the Prophet as if to thank him for having received Islam through him. Ibn Mashīsh sees in the historical Muḥammad an expression of the one Spirit from which all revelation comes and which is the eternal mediator between the ungraspable Godhead and the world. This is the Logos, the first manifestation of God and, as such, His universal symbol as well as His highest veil. By the very fact that in this way the Absolute reveals itself in a relative and multiple fashion, it also conceals itself. This eternal mediator is called the 'Muḥammadan Spirit' (*ar-Rūḥ al-Muḥammadī*), not because it is embodied only in Muḥammad—for all God's messengers and prophets manifest it—but because in the Islamic perspective Muḥammad is its most immediate expression. Divine Truth, the Sufis say, is in itself unlimited and inexhaustible, so that every religious form in which it deigns to clothe itself for the salvation of men can be no more than one possible form amongst others.

Sufi mysticism is predominantly founded on gnosis, and this finds expression in the saying of Abū'l-Ḥasan ash-Shādhilī: 'Know and be as thou wilt', he once said, and meant by this that the man who has realized what he is before God can do nothing else but act rightly.

He taught his disciples to look on the world with the eye of eternity: 'Attribute the actions of creatures to God as Agent; this will bring no harm to thee; whereas it will bring harm to thee if thou regardest creatures as the authors of their actions.' The spiritual attitude corresponding to this angle of vision is that of '*vacare Deo*', unconditional self-abandonment to God:

> The servant will not attain to God as long as he harbours any desire or ulterior motive. If thou wouldst please God, renounce thyself and thine environment and thy power over it. But this abandonment is not mere inaction: each moment is a sword, if thou cuttest not with it, it will cut thee (i.e. cause that moment to be lost for the remembrance of God).
>
> (*al-Madanī*)

Abū'l-Ḥasan ash-Shādhilī inaugurated a spiritual method for the acquiring of spiritual poverty and for the practising of it in the midst of worldly cares. Amongst the disciples that came to him during his lifelong peregrination from the Islamic West to the Islamic East, there were rich and poor, educated and uneducated, government ministers and day labourers.

His first successor was Abū'l-ʿAbbās al-Mursī, who lived in Egypt, and the one after that was the famous Aḥmad ibn ʿAṭā'illāh of Alexandria, whose 'Spiritual Aphorisms' (*Ḥikam*) became the breviary of almost everyone who followed the Sufi path, whether in the Far West (Morocco) or the Far East (Java and Sumatra). Ibn ʿAṭā'illāh died in 1309.

In addition to the Shādhilī line of spiritual masters who—like Aḥmad az-Zarrūq al-Barnūssī, born in Fez in 1441 and died in Tripoli in 1493—expounded Sufi doctrine with logical precision, there were always spiritual personalities who broke every rational framework, as if they incorporated some secret essence of the doctrine which transcended ordinary reason. One such was the master ʿAlī as-Sanhājī, who lived in Fez in the first half of the sixteenth century.

ᶜALĪ AS-SANHĀJĪ

The Shaykh ᶜAlī as-Sanhājī was known as the 'roamer', which can be understood in either a physical or a spiritual sense. For the people of Fez his holiness was as manifest as the morning star. He was a Fool of God in the style of the *Malāmatiyya* (those who intentionally draw people's criticism on themselves) and was constantly in the state of Divine attraction. He possessed neither home nor family. With his capacity for revealing what is hidden he could entirely see through those whom he met. He cared for neither praise nor blame. Thus he sometimes entered the houses of the Merinids, where women and children would crowd around him and kiss his hands and feet, without paying attention to anyone. They heaped on him costly clothes and jewelry, and the Sultan himself gave him garments of distinction. But he would go out and give away everything that he had received, and, in his fine garments, he would brush past the shops of oil merchants, so that they would become spotted with oil. During his constant roaming he increasingly invoked the name Allāh. No one knew where he lived. When he died, people swarmed to his funeral, and divided amongst themselves the planks from his bier, his prayer mat, and his clothes. He died in the year of the Hijra 950 (1542-43 A.D.) and was buried outside the Futūḥ gate. Even the Sultan and the scholars were present at his burial.

Amongst the miracles that people ascribe to him is the following: one day he stopped in front of a house, held up the lintel of the door with his hand, and shouted: 'O inhabitants of this house, come out, come out!' When all those who were inside had come out, he withdrew his hand, and the wall fell down.

On one occasion he suddenly entered the inner courtyard of a house, where a completely naked woman was washing her clothes. But he stretched out his arm, and caught a child who at that moment fell down from the roof. 'This is why I came in,' he said to the frightened woman, gave her the child, and left.

Once a Fez merchant, who was entering the Qarawiyyīn mosque for the morning prayer, saw him sitting on the threshold of the mosque eating cucumbers. It was market day (Thursday) and, as he said his prayer, the merchant considered how much he would offer for a donkey that he wished to buy. When he came out of the mosque he saw ᶜAlī as-Sanhājī still sitting on the threshold eating cucumbers. The merchant thought to himself: 'He would do better if, instead of eating cucumbers, he would say the morning prayer,' whereupon the Shaykh cried out to him: 'Better a cucumber-breakfast than a donkey-prayer!'

(*Salwāt al-Anfās*)

THE 'PATHS'

Every great master who has formulated the traditional Sufi path in a particular way thereby originated a spiritual 'path' or *ṭarīqa* for a particular category of human beings. A Sufi proverb says: 'The ways to God are as numerous as the souls of men.' Nevertheless there are particular categories of spiritual temperament and it is to these that the various 'paths' correspond.

As time passed, people who had chosen a particular path began to group together in spiritual brotherhoods, which sometimes also had an outward role. During the life-time of its founder, the centre of such an order was the founder's place of refuge or dwelling, and after his death, it was his tomb. Both of these were given the name of *zawiya*, which literally means corner, and is close to the old meaning of 'cell'. The sepulchral mosque, which often incorporated a pilgrim hostel, a Koran school, and sometimes a hospital, usually became the seat of the founder's successor and, as a centre of spiritual life, played a similar role for the Berber people as did the monasteries in early-medieval Europe for the Germanic and Celtic tribes.

The founder of an order very seldom nominated his successor. The successor usually emerged from amongst the surviving disciples because of his spiritual gifts. Nevertheless there was a fairly widespread tendency in the Maghrib to confer the succession to an outstanding spiritual master on one of his physical descendants. This was very much in keeping with the fact that most of the founders of orders in the Islamic West were themselves *shurafā'* (descendants of the Prophet). Amongst the Berbers *shurafā'* had for centuries been the bearers of the Islamic tradition, so that the role of the *sharifian* founders of orders must have seemed to them like a sudden actualization of the blessing that inheres in all the posterity of the Prophet, and as a confirmation of the genuineness of their descent. Good breeding and education were favourable for the spiritual succession, but they were not always enough. This is why it often happened that the family of a founder of an order retained only a formal authority, along with the administration of the sepulchral mosque, while real spiritual masters, who had manifested themselves within the order, took over the spiritual instruction and guidance.

As the Sufi orders spread amongst the people—and it sometimes happened that they penetrated whole tribes—it was in the nature of things that there should develop within them circles that aspired to take a more or less active part in the spiritual life. These circles increased all the more, since membership of an order did not preclude marriage or professional activity. In the immediate presence of the master there were usually a number of *fuqarā'* who completely renounced the world, and who found food and shelter in the *zawiya*; but most members of the order, whether men or women, were married.

AL-JAZŪLĪ

Towards the end of the fifteenth century and beginning of the sixteenth, Muḥammad Abū ᶜAbdallāh al-Jazūlī, a man from the far south of Morocco, founded a Shādhilī order. This order later played an important role in the defence of the Sūs against the Portuguese, which is why the Saadians brought the body of the founder to Marrakesh in order to inter it there.

Al-Jazūlī is famous throughout Morocco to this day for his work 'The Proofs of Goodness' (*Dalā'il al-khayrāt*), a collection of blessings on the Prophet in the form of a litany in which Muḥammad, the receptacle of revelation, appears as the summation of all the positive—and God-reflecting—aspects of creation.

From the spiritual posterity of al-Jazūlī several spiritual orders emerged which still exist in Morocco today. The most popular is undoubtedly the one founded in Meknes towards the end of the sixteenth century by the *sharīf* Muḥammad ben ᶜIsā al-Mukhtārī. It is related of this *sharīf* that he used his inherited wealth to recruit poor people who, for a daily wage, would invoke and praise God to the beating of drums. The Sultan, who found he was running short of labourers, forbade the unusual saint to continue this practice; but the saint simply moved with his followers to a cemetery and let it be said to the Sultan: 'Thou art the ruler of the living, but not of the dead; over them thou hast no authority.' These unusual beginnings may be the reason why the ᶜIsāwā brotherhood, apart from a small inner circle of men withdrawn from the world and entirely given over to ascesis and contemplation, has a large number of adherents who have become famous chiefly for their ecstatic dances—to magically powerful music—and for their so-called 'fakir' practices or accomplishments such as snake-charming and insensitivity to pain.

The ᶜAlawī Sultans, whose spiritual dignity likewise derived from their descent from the Prophet, were not always favourably disposed towards the *sharifian* heads of orders, who often had a strong influence on the people. Thus in the seventeenth century the Sultan Mulay Ismāᶜīl proceeded against the Shādhilī order that had been founded in 1660 by the Idrisite *sharīf* Mulay ᶜAbdallāh ben Ibrāhīm in Wazzān (Ouezzane), a small town to the north of Fez. This order also had a branch in Fez, which for many years was directed by an ascetic named Muḥammad al-Khayyāṭ. He was regarded as a saint, and after his death a cupola was erected over his grave. It is related that by appearing, after his death, to the Sultan he prevented the further persecution of the Wazzān order; one thing is certain: the ruler had to yield to the spiritual forces inherent in the order.

> The Sultan Mulay Ismāᶜīl, (writes al-Kattānī), issued a search order for Mulay Tuhāmī, the grandson of the founder. Mulay Tuhāmī, however, came from Wazzān to Meknes (the residence of the Sultan) and there entered the Green Mosque, so that the people feared for his safety. When, one morning, the Sultan had just had breakfast, and was thanking God for it, the Shaykh al-Khayyāṭ stepped into the alcove with a sharp sword in his hand, held it over the Sultan's head, and said: 'if a single hair of my master's son is harmed, I shall cut thee in pieces with this!' The Sultan asked: 'Who art thou then?' and he replied: 'Al-Khayyāṭ'. The Sultan asked further: 'And who is the son of thy master?' He replied: 'Mulay Tuhāmī who even now is in the Green Mosque.' Thereupon he

disappeared. The Sultan stood up and called for the guards on the doors; they maintained, however, that no one had got past them. Everyone in the house said the same: no one had seen the man with the sword. The Sultan became angry, called for his horse, and wanted to ride to the mosque. But the horse went backwards and would on no account allow itself to be driven forwards. At that the Sultan had Mulay Tuhāmī informed that he could return home, with God's peace. The the Sultan called for ᶜAbdallāh ar-Rūsī, the governor of Fez, and asked him: 'Is there in your city a man named al-Khayyāṭ?' 'Yes,' replied ar-Rūsī, 'he is buried in the Zarbatāna district and is called the lord of the valley.'

(*Salwāt al-Anfās*)

AṢ-ṢAQALLĪ

The link with the Islamic east was maintained by the pilgrims who travelled to Mecca. And thus it occurred that eastern spiritual orders like the Qādiriyya, the Khalwatiyya and the Naqshbandiyya spread to the Maghrib. In the middle of the eighteenth century a Fez man, from the noble family of the Ṣaqallī brought the Naqshbandī spiritual method from Egypt to Fez.

AT-TĪJĀNĪ

Towards the end of the eighteenth century Mulay Aḥmad at-Tījānī, who had studied in Fez and then lived for a long time in the east where he had contacts with the Khalwatiyya, founded a new order which henceforth was to bear his name. His doctrine and his method held the balance between the Sufi tradition and the generally accepted theology. For this reason his order always lived on the best terms with the ruling house. The principal centre of the order is ᶜAyn Māḍī in the south of Algeria, but the sepulchral mosque of the founder is in Fez, in the al-Blida district, where it is easily recognizable by its richly decorated doorway. Inside it is completely covered with blue and green arabesque mosaics. For a long time the order dominated the caravan routes through southern Algeria to the Sudan. It is well represented in Black Africa, and one can often meet Sudanese Muslims who have come to Fez to visit the tomb of the founder of the order.

AD-DARQĀWĪ

The pure Shādhilī tradition, which is representative of the earliest form of Sufism, was revivified at the end of the eighteenth century and the beginning of the nineteenth century by Mulay al-ᶜArabī ad-Darqāwī. His spiritual radiance extended well beyond the Maghrib. He was descended from a Ḥasanid family that lived amongst the Banū Zerwāl, in the hills to the north-east of Fez. As a young man he studied in Fez, and it was here too that he met his spiritual master, the Idrisid ᶜAlī al-Jamal, who roughly rebuffed him several times before accepting him as his disciple. In one of his letters, Mulay al-ᶜArabī tells how his master tested him by ordering him, a young scholar of noble lineage, to carry a load of fresh fruit through the town:

The first lesson that my master gave me was as follows: he ordered me to

> carry two baskets full of fresh fruit through the town. I carried them in my hands, and did not wish, as the others told me, to put them on my shoulders, for that was unwelcome to me, and constricted my soul, so that it became agitated and fearful, and grieved beyond measure, till I almost began to weep. And, by God, I still had to weep for all the shame, humiliation, and scorn that I had to undergo as a result! Never before had my soul had to suffer such a thing, so I was not conscious of its pride and cowardice. I had not known whether it was proud or not, since no professor, amongst all those that I had frequented, had ever taught me about my soul. While I was in this state, my master, who perceived my pride and my inner distress, came up to me, took the two baskets from my hands, and placed them on my shoulders with the words: 'Distinguish thus between good and evil.' Thereby he opened the door for me and led me on the right way, for I learned to discriminate between the proud and the humble, the good and the bad, the wise and the foolish, the orthodox and the heretical, between those who know and translate their knowledge into deeds, and those who do not. From that moment no orthodox person ever overpowered me with his orthodoxy, no heretic with his heresy, no scholar with his knowledge, no pious man with his piety, and no fasting man with his asceticism. For my master, may God have mercy on him, had taught me to distinguish truth from vanity, and wheat from chaff. (*Rasā'il*)

Later his master entrusted him with the task of teaching and revivifying the Shādhilī spiritual method which had become almost completely forgotten. He wrote as follows to certain of his disciples:

> The extraordinary Shādhilī way, on which our master journeyed—may God be pleased with him—is what you have deviated from. Whether he bequeathed this way to you or not, what does it matter? For you now follow another way. And if you should ask me, how is this so? Then I would answer: his way consisted in climbing down and not in climbing up, but your way consists in climbing up and not in climbing down. His way was outwardly humiliation and inwardly ascension, whereas your way is outwardly ascension and inwardly descent. One can also say that his way was outwardly a way of rigour and discipline, and inwardly a way of grace and beauty, whereas your way, like that of most people, is beautiful on the outside and servitude on the inside. And may God forbid that the way of the elect be like that of the multitude! It is likewise not the business of those who are spiritually aware to content themselves with the recitation of litanies, and you do nothing else but that. Moreover, one should have one sole spiritual master and not several, as you do. That is what I have perceived of your situation, and I therefore suspect that your little barque has no wind in its sails . . . (*Rasā'il*)

His instruction went straight to the heart of the matter, and in this way illumined both learned and unlearned, scholars and Bedouins. The following are further extracts from his letters, which his disciples collected and later, towards the beginning of the nineteenth century, published in a lithographed edition in Fez.

> The *fuqarā'* of ancient times sought only for what could kill their souls (*nufūs* plural of *nafs*) and bring life to their hearts, whereas we do just the opposite. We seek after that which kills our hearts and enlivens our souls. They strove only to become free of their passions and dethrone their ego; but, for us, what we long for is the satisfaction of our sensual desires and the glorification of our ego, and thus we have turned our backs to the door and our faces to the wall. I say this to you only because I have seen the favours which God lavishes on him who kills his soul and enlivens his heart. Most certainly we are satisfied with less, but only the ignorant are satisfied with not arriving at the end of the journey.
>
> I asked myself whether there could be something else, apart from our passions and our egoism, which cuts us off from the divine gifts, and as a third hindrance I found the lack of spiritual longing. For intuition is generally given only to him whose heart is pierced by an intense longing and a strong desire to contemplate the Essence of his Lord. Intuitions of the Divine Essence flow into such a man until he is extinguished in that Essence and thus freed from the illusion of any reality other that It, for this is the direction in which the Divine Essence leads those whose gaze is continually fixed upon It. On the contrary, he who aspires exclusively to theoretical knowledge, or to outward action, does not receive intuition upon intuition; he would not rejoice in it if he did, since his wish is aimed at something other than the Divine Essence, and God (may He be exalted) favours each one according to the measure of his aspiration. Certainly, every man participates in the Spirit, just as the ocean has waves, but sensual experience entirely takes possession of most men; it seizes hold of their hearts and limbs and does not allow them to open to the Spirit, because sensuality is the opposite of spirituality and opposites do not meet.
>
> We see besides that the spiritual aim is reached neither by many works, nor by few, but by Grace alone. As the saint Ibn ʿAṭā'illāh says in his Aphorisms, (*Ḥikam*): 'If you were destined to reach Him only after the destruction of your faults and the abandonment of all your claims, you would never reach Him. But when He wishes to bring you back towards Him, He absorbs your quality into His and your attributes into His and thus brings you back by means of what comes to you from Him, not by means of what comes to Him from you.'
>
> One of the effects of Divine Bounty, Grace, and Generosity is that one

finds the Master who can grant spiritual education; without Divine Grace no one would find or recognize him, since, according to the saying of the saint Abū'l-ᶜAbbās al-Mursī (may God be pleased with him): 'It is more difficult to know a saint than to know God.' Again, in the *Ḥikam* of Ibn ᶜAṭā'illāh, it is said: 'Exalted be He who makes His saints known only in order to make Himself known and who leads towards them those whom He wishes to lead towards Himself.'

The heart of man cannot attach itself to the Divine Essence unless his ego has been effaced, extinguished, destroyed, annihilated . . . As the saint Abū Madyan has said: 'Whoever does not die, does not see God.' All the masters of our way have taught the same. And take care that you do not think that it is the things of the body and the soul that veil God from us. By God, what veils Him is nothing other than illusion, and illusion is vain. As the saint Ibn ᶜAṭā'illāh has said: 'God did not veil Himself from thee by some reality coexisting with Him, since there is no reality other than He. What veils Him from thee is naught but the illusion that something outside Him could possess any reality.' . . .

Know that the *faqīr* can only kill his soul when he has been able to see its form, and he will only see its form when he has separated himself from the world, from his companions, from his friends, and from his habits.

One *faqīr* said to me: 'My wife has got the better of me.' To which I answered: 'It is not she but your own soul that has got the better of you; we have no other enemy; if thou couldst dominate thy soul, thou wouldst dominate the whole world—not merely thy wife.' . . .

The soul is something immense; it is the whole cosmos since it is a copy of it. Everything that is in the cosmos is in the soul and everything that is in the soul is in the cosmos. Therefore, whoever masters his soul masters the world, and whoever is mastered by his soul is mastered by the world. . . .

Spiritual intuition is very subtle. It can only be fixed spatially by concrete symbols and temporally by interior prayer (*dhikr*), holy company, and the breaking of habits. . . .

All things are hidden in their opposites—gain in loss, gift in refusal, honour in humiliation, wealth in poverty, strength in weakness, abundance in restriction, rising up in falling down, life in death, victory in defeat, power in powerlessness, and so on. Therefore, if a man wish to find, let him be content to lose; if he wish a gift, let him be content with refusal; he who desires honour must accept humiliation, and he who desires wealth must be satisfied with poverty; let him who wishes to be strong be content to be weak; let him who wishes abundance be resigned to restriction; he who wishes to be raised up must allow himself to be cast down; he who desires life must accept death; he who wishes to conquer must be content with impotence . . . (*Rasā'il*)

Mulay al-ᶜArabī ad-Darqāwī had a large number of disciples in Fez, but he finally left the city, and founded a hermitage at Bu Berih, a remote spot in the Banū Zerwāl hills, between Fez and the Rif mountains. There he died in 1823, when several of his disciples were already active as masters in different parts of the Maghrib.

The late Mohammed Bu Shaᶜara, Muqaddim of the Darqāwī order founded by Mulay al-ᶜArabī ad-Darqāwī (c.1743–1823).

AL-ᶜALAWĪ

A great Shādhilī master in the first part of the present century was the Algerian Shaykh Aḥmad ben Muṣṭafā al-ᶜAlawī, who had many disciples in Morocco, as well as in the Near East, Southern Arabia, India, and Java.

Under the French protectorate, the Sufi orders, which constitute large and therefore politically important communities, encountered ever increasing difficulties. To preserve their liberty, the heads of orders were compelled to show proof of their approval of the European administration, which made them guilty of treason in the eyes of the younger generation who were striving for national independence. Many true masters withdrew entirely from public life. Thus Mulay ᶜAlī remained silent, and Mulay aṣ-Ṣiddīq, of whom we spoke earlier, hid himself under the mask of a fool. Another important master of that time, Muḥammad at-Tādilī, who lived at Magazan but often came to Fez, refrained from founding a *zawiya*, but frequented circles of *fuqarā'* here and there in order to counteract the spiritual laziness that had already become apparent.

Later he became blind and paralysed, but at the time that I made his acquaintance in Fez, between the two world wars, he was still at the height of his powers, a giant physically and spiritually, although his eyes which were already afflicted by a disease, almost always remained closed: this made his features, which were reminiscent of an Assyrian king, look all the more recollected. When he spoke of spiritual matters, his speech, with its characteristic Arabic sounds, seemed to sparkle with flashes from an inexhaustible inward fire.

Muḥammad at-Tādilī used to scold the members of the Sufi orders in Fez: 'You imagine,' he would say to them, 'that you have attained something on the spiritual way, because you perform many exercises. But as long as you cannot speak about spiritual truths spontaneously and with a full heart, you have tasted nothing' And on another occasion he said: 'Most of these people spend their lives in mosques and *zawiyas* sitting beside the Divine bride (the Truth, *al-ḥaqīqa*), but alas they sit with her back to back!'

Once when he was staying in the house of a Fez merchant, where I was also a guest, someone asked him what was the meaning of the Koranic verse: '*He created the two seas that meet together, between them an isthmus they do not overpass.*' He immediately interpreted the verse as an image of the relationship between two degrees of reality: of one of the two seas, the Koran says that it is sweet and pleasant to taste, and of the other, that it is salty and bitter. The purity and sweetness indicate a higher level of reality, while the bitterness indicates a relatively lower level, one more strongly mixed with 'nothingness'. The isthmus (*barzakh*) between the two seas or degrees of reality separates them, but at the same time unites them, like the narrow neck of an hourglass or like a lens that concentrates the sun's rays and then transmits them again, but inverted. Whenever two domains of reality meet there is an isthmus of this kind. Applied to man, the sweet sea means the pure Intellect or Spirit (*ar-Rūḥ*), which in itself is undivided and capable of direct knowledge; while the bitter sea is the psyche (*an-nafs*), which is troubled and dissipated by passions. The isthmus is the Heart (*Qalb*). The psyche cannot 'overpass' the threshold of the Heart. Bound as it is to imaginings and tendencies, the psyche cannot lay hold on the Spirit that transcends all forms, and in this sense the isthmus divides the two seas. But the Spirit or Intellect is able, not to remove the isthmus, but, through the Heart, to act upon the psyche. It confers its light on the psyche, just as the physical heart confers life on the body. The heart opens itself to this all-radiant light by means of the remembrance of God. Without this the spiritual pulse becomes weak and the soul sinks into opaqueness . . . Taking this interpretation as his starting-point, Shaykh Tādilī expounded the whole ladder of existence up to the 'isthmus' between the created and the Uncreated, and then down again to the various isthmuses between individual faculties of the soul and the external world. When he began, it was already late evening; the light of morning was visible when he concluded his discourse—which had frequently been interspersed by long silences. His listeners, however, had the impression that it had only lasted for a moment.

Once a year, on Mulay al-ᶜArabī's birthday, members of his order make a pilgrimage to his grave and that of his son and successor Mulay aṭ-Ṭayyib, in the hills to the north of Fez. On one such occasion, I joined a group of pilgrims who made their way on foot northwards up the inhospitable hillside overgrown with dark bushes, past creviced slopes from which sand constantly slid down to the depths below. They walked in single file along the crest of the hills, with staffs in their hands and their white burnouses thrown back over their shoulders. As they came closer to their destination they could see on other hills similar white-clad groups making their way upwards in single file and could hear their half-plaintive, half-jubilant song, consisting of the words of the attestation of faith: 'There is no divinity other than God!'

In the meantime, the sun had risen quite high; the shadows shortened under the bushes, which lay like a panther's spots on the yellow and red desert. Soon the vault of heaven seemed to attain white-heat, and the light fell down so straight that near and far became as one.

During the afternoon the hills became rounder again—and more menacing too, like countless wild animals pressing themselves against the blue-green edge of the sky. Here and there near the top, grew evergreen oaks. The pilgrims continued their way through this timeless landscape, as if they already walked on the other side of death, or along the partition separating the two worlds, and their song rose, harsh and clear, like a song of victory over death.

At the head of the procession went a few old men with wrinkled and weathered features. With their turbans and white face-veils, they looked as if they were wrapped up like mummies. As I looked up at the white-clad, half-bent figures climbing the red hill ahead of me, they made me think of souls ascending the mount of Purgatory.

Towards evening, a wide valley opened up in front of us, where, in a clearing in the oak forest, we could see a few bright houses of whitewashed mud, surrounded by fields of wheat. This was the hermitage of Mulay at-Ṭayyib, which had now grown into a village. Opposite, on a hillock between two oaks, rose the grey-white cupola that covered the tomb of the master. As with countless other saints' tombs in Islam, the hemispherical dome, slightly raised at the top, rested on a simple square room. Square and circle, cube and sphere—here they were so perfectly matched, that they reconciled heaven and earth and, by their harmony, charmed and blessed surrounding nature.

As we came nearer, the dome of the saint's tomb rose like a full moon over the dark oaks and against the green-gold evening sky. Swallows darted and twittered around the starkly plain building, on which the lime was crumbling with age. The heavy cedar door was open. The inside was empty except for a black oak shrine above the grave. A few inscriptions were carved in the wood, including the Koranic verses: *Think not that those who have been killed in the way of God are dead; no, they are alive . . . Those who believe and whose hearts are at rest in the remembrance of God. Verily in the remembrance of God do hearts find rest . . . No fear oppresses them and no care.*

The white light in the small sepulchral room, the solitude of the place, and the intensity of fervour which filled it, were like a cool radiance, comparable to pure snow from which a living stream flowed.

The dervishes, who themselves were disciples of disciples of the master buried here, walked into the wooden shrine, touched it with their hands, and prayed softly. Amongst them were townsmen and countrymen, Arabs and Berbers, men and women. Led by an elderly woman, a group of Berber women from the mountains, unveiled and carrying large wooden rosaries, approached the tomb. They were enshrouded in woollen blankets with coloured fringes, and with their yellowish faces they reminded me of American Indians. The faces of all the pilgrims, whether young or old, sophisticated townsmen or simple country people, displayed the same gentle radiance.

In the house in which Mulay aṭ-Ṭayyib had once lived, his son Mulay ᶜAlī awaited us. Inside the long rooms made of sun-dried brick and arranged in a semi-circle which constituted the farmyard, we were encompassed in that simple clarity that had often enchanted me in Moroccan peasant houses: the whitewashed and slightly curved walls, the floors of flattened earth, the light structure of the ceiling; rafters of knotty wood forming a long gable that ran above our heads like the upturned hull of a boat. One felt that one had found refuge, as if in a boat for living in, and that one was surrounded by peace. There was nothing in the room that could distract one's mind; it had almost no furniture, only a mat, an amphora with drinking water which stood in a recess in the floor, a candlestick, and a leather hassock. In surroundings such as these, human gestures became meaningful and full of dignity.

'A house for the wild men of the mountains,' said Mulay ᶜAlī laughing, 'but it is all one needs. This water comes from a pure spring that my father dug out a little down the hillside. On the few slopes that you see around us, and in another valley that we made arable, we grew our bread. Everything else is either pasture for goats, or wilderness. When my father constructed this room, in order to live with his family in solitude, the place was still completely surrounded by woods. At night the wild boar and the lynx would rub against the walls. Then, as more and more disciples and followers continued to arrive, the clearing, the village, and the arable land slowly began to develop. The influence of my forefathers continued to grow. Lower in the valley more villages were founded, and the whole tribe of mountain-dwellers from all around followed the instruction that emanated from here . . . that is, until the French arrived.'

In the morning of the next day the dervishes gathered in a clearing in the woods near the tomb. The clearing was on a piece of raised ground, and on it one was at the level of the surrounding tree-tops. There must have been a thousand men there, and, holding hands, they formed several concentric circles. In the middle, a space the size of a threshing floor contained a group of singers. The men in the circles intoned the name of God, in an increasingly rapid rhythm, while their bodies moved up and down. The enunciation of the Divine Name slowly changed into a deep breathing, and finally into a kind of death-rattle.

The singers, with voices as bright as flutes, sang an elegy to divine knowledge, personified as a woman, Laylā, that was written by Shaykh Muḥammad al-Ḥarrāq, a disciple of Mulay al-ᶜArabī:

Thou seekest Laylā. Yet she manifesteth herself within thee.
Thou deemest her to be elsewhere, but elsewhere existeth not.
That is a madness, well-known to lovers.
So be on your guard, for otherness is the epitome of separation.
Seest thou not, how her beauty enfoldeth thee.
She disappeareth only if thou refusest part of thee.
Come close to me, thou sayst to her, to her who is thine All.
And when she loveth thee, she leadeth thee to thyself.
Bliss ineffable is the meeting with her.
No one reacheth her, who knoweth not essence without form.
I have dissimulated about her,
After I had truly displayed her through my veil.
I hid her from myself, with the garment of mine own existence,
And, out of jealousy, I hid her from the envier.
Dazzling beauty! Should the light of thy countenance
Touch the eyes of a blind man, he would see each particle of dust.
She is adorned with every grace pertaining unto beauty.
And wherever she appeareth, she is desired by those who love.
(*Diwān al-Ḥarrāq*)

The dancers' eyes were closed, their bodies weightless. Their faces seemed to be turned inwards, like the faces of the dying. Their souls seemed already to have departed from their bodies. Indeed it seemed as if their bodies had been grasped by their souls, and lifted powerfully upwards. The breathing of all present was like one single breath, and became more and more rapid, so that finally air, earth, and surrounding trees all seemed to join in the same rhythm. The space between heaven and earth on which the dancers stood had become like a bellows. The corporeal world seemed to have been absorbed by the world of the soul, whose reality now began to break through, just as when the unity of the soul suddenly grips the breath of a dying man, the pulse of a lover, or the body of a butterfly awakening into life.

Above the rhythmical breathing the song rang out and floated, almost motionlessly, through the air, like a falcon planing, almost motionlessly, above his prey. Now and again a word from the song would pierce one particular heart, and the dancer, whose heart had been struck by the lightning of spiritual realization, fell unconscious to the ground. An old man, who walked amongst the dancers, would cover him with a burnous.

Along with Mulay ʿAlī we went further up to mountainside, and saw, from above, the circle of dancing men. 'Do you think these dervishes have lost their reason?' he asked smiling. 'What they do is good,' he went on, 'for it derives from a saying of the Prophet: "Whoever does not leap when he hears the name of his friend, does not really have a friend." Then he added earnestly: 'But how easily the senses are misled and the intention deflected. All that you have seen is not yet the way that leads to the Knowledge of God, as the Sufi masters taught it!' 'What then is this way?' I asked. He pointed with his hand towards the blinding sun: 'It is like that', he said, 'and it is also like Christ's injunction to offer the left cheek to him who strikes you on the right.'

Members of a Sufi brotherhood.

8 The Irruption of the Modern World

In MEDIEVAL SPAIN Muslims, Christians and Jews lived side by side in peace, apart from occasions when there might be political tensions between them. For the Moorish rulers this situation was a natural one, as toleration of Jews and Christians has its root in Islamic law; however the Christian kings, for whom this law did not operate, also frequently granted their Muslim and Jewish subjects the same right. This was in no wise the result of religious indifferentism, for in those days faith took precedence over all else. It seems that it was experience which led to this mutual respect, to the presentiment that behind the strange appearances of another religious form the same divine Truth was to be found, and a willingness to leave judgement on this matter to God. Moreover, in spite of the three dogmatic systems which distinguished the communities from one another, the spiritual world in which they lived was virtually the same: life and death, heaven and earth, knowledge and crafts, had for each of them the same meaning and value. It is significant that the spiritual exchange between the Islamic and Christian worlds broke off suddenly with the rationalism of the Renaissance, and that at the same time the intolerance of the absolute Spanish monarchy began: the Jews were forcibly converted or persecuted, and the Moors expelled.

From then on the Islamic West shut itself off from Christian Europe, and when, much later, in the nineteenth century, it was compelled to enter again into relations with European states, they no longer confronted it as Christian nations, but as something quite different, and wholly foreign to the Muslim way of thinking.

What the Moroccans, who at that time made the acquaintance of Europe, thought of modern civilization, can be gleaned from a conversation quoted by the author Edmondo de Amicis in his report on the journey of an Italian ambassador to Fez in 1879:

> Today I had a lively discussion with a merchant in Fez with a view to finding out what the Moors think of European civilization . . . He was a fine man, about forty years old, with an honest and serious face, who had made business visits to the most important cities in Western Europe and had lived for a long time in Tangier, where he learnt Spanish . . . I asked him therefore what kind of impression the large cities of Europe had made on him . . . He looked hard at me and answered coldly: 'Large streets, fine shops, beautiful palaces, good workshops, everything clean.' He gave the impression that with these words, he had mentioned everything in our countries that was worthy of praise. 'Have you not found anything else in Europe that is beautiful and good?' I asked. He looked at me questioningly. 'Is it possible,' I went on, 'that an intelligent man like you, who has visited several countries so marvellously superior to your own, can speak about them without astonishment, or at least without the emotion of a country boy who has seen the pasha's palace? What can you possibly admire in the world? What sort of people are you? Who can possibly understand you?' '*Perdone Usted,*' he answered coldly, 'it is for me to say that I cannot understand you. I have told you all the things which I consider to be better in Europe. What more can I say? Have I to say something that I do not believe to be true? I repeat that your streets are larger than ours, your shops finer, that you have workshops such as we do not have, and also rich palaces. That is all. I can only add one more thing: that you know more than we do, because you have many books, and read more.' I became impatient. 'Do not lose patience, *Caballero,*' he said, 'let us speak together calmly. Is not a man's first duty honesty? Is it not honesty more than anything else that makes a man worthy of respect, and one country superior to another? Very well, then. As far as honesty is concerned, your countries are certainly not better than ours. That much I can say right away.' 'Gently, gently!' I said, 'Tell me first what you mean by honesty!' 'Honesty in business, *Caballero*. The Moors, for example, sometimes cheat the Europeans in trade, but you Europeans cheat the Moors much more often.' 'There must be a few cases,' I replied, in order to say something. '*Casos raros?*' he exclaimed angrily. 'It happens every day! Proof: I go to Marseilles. I buy cotton. I choose a particular thread, give the

exact reference number and brand-name, as well as the amount required. I ask for it to be sent, I pay, and I return home. Back in Morocco, I receive the cotton. I open the consignment, and take a look. I find the same number, the same brand-name, and a thread that is of one third the thickness! This is anything but good, and I lose thousands of francs! I rush to the consulate, but in vain. Another case: A merchant from Fez places an order in Europe for blue cloth, so many pieces, of such and such a length and breadth. He pays for it when the bargain is made. In due course he receives the cloth, opens the package, and checks the measurements. The first pieces are all right, those underneath are shorter, and those lowest down are half a metre too short! The cloth cannot be used for cloaks, and the merchant is ruined . . . And so on and so on!' He raised his eyes upwards, and turned to me and said: 'So you are more honest than we are?' I repeated that it could only be a matter of individual cases. He said nothing, and then suddenly exclaimed: 'Are you more pious than we are? No! . . . One needs only to have visited your "mosques" once . . . Tell me,' he continued, since I remained silent, 'are there in your country fewer murders?' I could not bring myself to answer. How could I have admitted that in Italy alone there are three thousand murders a year, and that there are nineteen thousand people in prison, convicted and not yet convicted. 'I do not think there are,' he said, reading the answer in my eyes.

As I could feel no confidence in this area, I turned to him with the customary objection about polygamy. He jumped up as if stung. 'So it's that again', he exclaimed, blushing to the roots of his hair. 'As if you Europeans only had one woman! Don't try to make us believe that! One is indeed your own, but then there are those '*de los otros*' and those '*de todos y nadie*'. Paris! London! The coffee-houses, the streets, the theatres are full of them. *Vergüenza*! And you criticize the Moors!' As he spoke, he fingered his rosary with a trembling hand, and sometimes turned to me with a smile, as if to say that his indignation was not directed at me personally but at Europe. Since my question had obviously embarrassed him, I changed the subject, and referred to the comforts of European civilization . . . 'That is true,' he replied. 'A bit of sun? A sunshade! Rain? An umbrella! Dust? A pair of gloves! Walking? A walking-stick! Looking around? Eye glasses. An excursion? A coach! Sitting down? A chair! Eating? Knives and forks! A scratch? A doctor! Death? A statue! You want for nothing! Are you really men? '*Por Dios*', you are infants!' He even made fun of our architecture, when I spoke to him about the comfort of our houses. 'What? Three hundred of you live in a single building, all on top of one another! You have to climb, climb, climb . . . There is no air, no light, and no garden!'

I now spoke to him about our laws, our governments, and similar

> things, and since he was an intelligent man, I thought I would at last manage to give him a glimpse of the immense difference between my country and his. Since in this sector he could not hold his own, he changed the subject of the conversation, and suddenly said with a smile, looking me up and down from head to foot! '*Mal vestidos* (badly dressed)'. I replied that dress was of no importance, but added that in this domain too he would surely acknowledge our superiority, for instead of idly sitting cross-legged for hours, we employed our time in thousands of useful or entertaining pursuits. To this he gave a more subtle answer than I had expected: it did not seem a good sign to him, he said, that we felt the need to do so many things in order to pass the time. Life itself must be torture for us, if we were totally unable to sit still for a single hour, without being killed by boredom and having to seek relief in some distraction or conversation. Were we afraid of ourselves? What was it that tormented us? . . .
>
> I now spoke of the European industries, the railways, the telegraph, and all the great public works. He let me speak without interruption, and even nodded his head from time to time. But when I finished, he sighed and said: 'all very well, but what use are these things when we all must die?' 'In brief,' I said, 'you would not exchange your situation for ours?' He thought a little and then replied: 'No, for you do not live longer than we do, you are not healthier, nor better, nor more pious, nor happier. Leave us then in peace. Do not wish that everyone should live as you do and be happy according to your lights. Let us both live in the milieu in which God has placed us. It is not for nothing that God has put a sea between North Africa and Europe. Let us respect His ordinance!' 'So you believe,' I said, 'that you will always remain as you are, that we shall not gradually succeed in compelling you to change?' 'I do not know,' he replied: 'you have the power; you will do what you will. But everything that has to happen is already written by God. And whatever it is that must happen, God will not forsake those who remain faithful to Him.' With these words, he took my right hand, pressed it to his heart, and walked away majestically . . . (*de Amicis*)

The European intervention in Morocco took place more or less suddenly. At the beginning it had for the Moroccans a purely military character, which they could understand, and which was not completely devoid of heroic aspects. Completely other, however, was the administrative subjugation of Morocco. Lyautey, who was appointed as French Resident-General in Morocco, wrote in 1912 about the meaning of the state treaty, by means of which France's protectorate over Morocco was recognized: 'A country under protectorate status retains its own institutions. It rules itself through its own organs, and is simply supervised by the European power, which takes its place in external relations, in its political dealings with other states.' For Morocco, this meant that its theocratic form of government and the traditional structure of its society should remain the same, at least internally. But, in the same report, Lyautey continues: 'The protecting power takes over in general responsibility for the army and the finances of the country under protection, and guides it as regards its economic development.' And this opened the door to interference in every domain of native life. General Lyautey's own intention was that, as far as possible, Morocco should be governed through its own élite. He repeatedly declared: 'The relationship in question (the protectorate) means supervision, and not direct administration.' Unfortunately his aristocratic conception of what a protectorate implied was vastly different both from that of the French officials who, as citizens of a secular state looked on the traditional institutions of Morocco with mistrust and distaste, and from that of the European settlers who wished to acquire land. This is why Lyautey declared at Lyons in 1916:

> Morocco is not like Algeria. There we found only loose sand and no organic structure. The only power was that of the Turkish Dey, and this crumbled when we arrived. In Morocco, on the other hand, we are faced with a historic and independent empire, jealous in the extreme of its independence, and resistant to any form of servitude. Until a year or two ago it was a properly constituted state, with a hierarchy of officials, with diplomatic representation abroad, and with its own social institutions, most of which still exist, in spite of the recent collapse of central authority. Do not forget that there are still, in Morocco, a goodly number of personages who until six years ago were the ambassadors of their country at St. Petersburg, London, Berlin, Madrid, and Paris, accompanied by secretaries and attachés, all men of general culture who were perfectly capable of dealing on an equal footing with European statesmen . . .
>
> Alongside this political establishment there also exists a religious establishment, which is anything but negligible. The Sultan's present Minister of Justice was a distinguished professor successively at the Universities of al-Azhar (Cairo), Istanbul, Bursa and Damascus, and is in correspondence with *ᶜulemā* (Islamic jurists) as far afield as India, and he is by no means the only one who maintains relations with the Islamic élite in the East.
>
> Finally, there is a first class economic team, composed of the leading merchants, who have branches in Manchester and Marseilles, and who in most instances have been to these branches in person.
>
> We are therefore confronted with three élites: political, religious and economic. It would be madness to ignore them and to fail to seek their aid; for if we make them our allies, they can powerfully help us in the task we have to accomplish. Let us remember—and those of you who have been to Morocco know it full well—that the people there are industrious,

> conscientious and open to progress and the more we respect what is sacred to them, the more we shall receive in return. This country, then, offers us the most favourable circumstances for accomplishing a great work, in cooperation with the native inhabitants, on condition that we completely abandon all the prejudices and maladroitness that have so gravely harmed us elsewhere, and that we shun like the plague the contemptible state of mind that is summed up in the phrase *sale bicot*, applied indiscriminately to all natives, an expression not only shocking but dangerous, and in its contempt and its menace, only too well understood by those to whom it is addressed, giving rise in them to a bitterness which nothing will efface, as I have so often, alas, had occasion to observe.
>
> No other country is better suited to this concept of protectorate, a concept which is definitive and not transitory . . . Annexation or 'colonization' would immediately and automatically involve the imposition of French law. Overnight the French administration with its inflexible stucture, its power to drag its feet, and its heaviness, would come crashing down on the unfortunate country . . . Nothing, I assure you, less resembles the suburbs of Guingamp or Trévoux than Fez or Marrakesh. (*Paroles d'Action*)

Lyautey's conception of the role of the French in Morocco presupposed a certain understanding of traditional Islamic culture, which very few officials had, apart from himself, and for which the ordinary education of the Europeans who came to Morocco was scarcely a preparation. Lyautey recalls an experience of his own:

> At the Fez Fair in 1916, which coincided with the Prophet's birthday, and at which the Sultan himself was present, a highly placed French official, not familiar with Morocco, said to me: 'Well, I think I have understood your policy. I can see how useful it is to conserve intact this form of government, all these archaic and out-of-date things, as long as we are at war. That is very wise. But it is obvious, is it not, to you as well as to me, that as soon as peace comes, all that must be swept away, to make room for good direct administration, on the model of the Metropolis, and more and more resembling a French *département*.' My reply was perhaps a trifle summary, and I shall repeat it here even more briefly: 'The Sultan, his officials and all the traditional institutions of Morocco are no mere façade . . . None of these things must be "swept away", because it cannot be done and may not be done . . . If the bi-lateral pact binds us to the Sultan, it also binds us to the people . . . In my whole soul, and on the basis of my experience, I am convinced that in this country one serves

> France best by winning the heart of the people for it . . . That is the quintessence of this policy of "protectorate" . . . Out of love for my own country, I express the wish that my successors shall also remain true to this policy . . .' That he was disappointed in this hope can clearly be seen from his admonitory proclamation of 1920: 'In Morocco we are in no way faced with a primitive, barbaric, or passive population . . . Nothing could be more dangerous than that the European settlers in this country should commit imprudences, for which one will later have to pay dearly; nothing is more dangerous than causing the germs of discontent and disquiet, already present in this people, to grow . . . The Moroccans are desirous of knowledge and very adaptable. There is a youth amongst them that is keen to live and to achieve, and that has a taste for knowledge and trade. In the absence of opportunity and scope, which our administration offers them only so grudgingly and at the lowest level, they will seek other outlets; they will attach themselves to whatever European societies they come in contact with . . . or they will turn to foreign Islamic societies, and in the end they will unite together in order to achieve their demands for themselves . . . I am fully aware where the practical problems lie . . . Above all, all of us, whether we be officials from France or officers from Algeria, have "direct rule" in our blood. And in everything relating to the administration, all of us, to a greater or lesser degree, have the tendency to look on the "natives" as inferior and as a negligible factor.'
>
> (*Paroles d'Action*)

In 1921 the revolt led by ʿAbd al-Krim broke out in the Rif Mountains in the Spanish Moroccan protectorate. It spread to the French protectorate and was suppressed only after a war of several years waged by France and Spain together. In 1924 or 1925 there was even, for a while, the danger that the warring Rif Kabyles might succeed in establishing contact with the unsubdued Berber tribes in the south, and so bring about an encirclement of central Morocco, including Fez.

When the French army in Morocco finally 'pacified' the Kabyles in the North and the insubordinate tribes in the Atlas, the protectorate authorities, in 1930, issued an official decree, according to which the Berbers were no longer subject to the canonical and basically Koranic jurisdiction, but were to receive their own system of justice based on tribal custom. The French government, who had planned the move, were of the opinion that the majority of the Berbers had embraced Islam only superficially and as a result of Arab pressure. By freeing them from canon law, and thereby also from the need to learn Arabic, it was hoped that they could be detached from the oriental and traditional culture of Islam, and won over to the European civilization of France.

But the 'Berber Decree' (*dahir berbère*), of 1930 provoked an indignant resistance from both Arabs and Berbers. The Berbers clearly saw in it an attempt to separate them from the community of Islam, and the Arab or Arabized population saw the decree as a betrayal of the Protectorate Agreement of 1912, according to which the French had the right to subdue the warring Berbers, not on their own behalf, but in the name of the Sultan, and for his jurisdiction.

The indignation of the Berber population led to the creation of a committee which, in 1934, demanded the honest implementation of the Protectorate Agreement with France. When the French government refused to meet this demand in any way, a political resistance movement was set up, the goal of which was complete independence for Morocco. It was formed largely by the youth of the cities, who were already more or less influenced by modern political ideology. Whether this ideology came via Turkey and Egypt, or arose because of French education, it was in any case of European origin, so that in the last analysis it was Europe itself that undermined its own domination in North Africa. The older generation were in general mistrustful with regard to this movement. They knew only too well that political independence for Morocco could not come about without its transformation into a modern state, equipped with technical means; and this meant the loss of all traditional forms of life.

Many young townspeople were under the influence of the 'Salafiya' movement, which originated in Egypt, and which sought to adapt Islamic law to the modern way of life by elements of European rationalism: instead of tradition, there should be a free interpretation of the Koran. The treaty of alliance between the head of the community and the responsible doctors of the law was to be replaced by universal suffrage. Instead of the unity of the world of Islam, there should be an aspiration for 'Arab unity'.

As the Sultan Mohammed V inclined more and more towards the independence movement of the city youth, the French administration tried to play the tribes of the Atlas, who had remained cool towards the predominantly Arab liberation movement, against the throne. This was only half successful. The people saw through the stratagem and, although the Sultan was obliged to yield, it was precisely because of his humiliation that the French Protectorate authorities lost almost entirely the confidence of the population.

The oscillating attitude subsequently exhibited by the French authorities was the result of an inward contradiction that had been present from the beginning: those progressive-minded Moroccans, from whom the European rulers now had most to fear, were the very ones who were ideologically closest to them, while the traditional circles, whom they needed to help them maintain the status quo, were for them spiritually foreign. They could not use them for their own ends without at the same time destroying them and undermining them in their traditional role.

When a series of uprisings broke out in the cities in 1953, the French Resident-General had the Sultan deposed and exiled. A new Sultan was to be appointed by a gathering of tribal leaders and heads of orders, who represented the traditional and anti-modernist section of the population. They appointed another ʿAlawite noble called Muḥammad ben ʿArafa; but it immediately became clear that the traditional dignitaries who made the choice had no real support amongst the people for, according to Islamic custom, it is not the tribal leaders, but the doctors of the law who, by their oath of allegiance, put the seal of legitimacy on the choice of a caliph. Henceforth the tribal chiefs, *caïds*, and heads of orders concerned were regarded as the puppets of the foreign rulers. Under a protectorate, any dignity that is not accompanied by effective power is necessarily undermined. By going through with the sham spectacle of a sacred enthronement of the new Sultan, the French merely dissipated what remained of the respect that the people had been willing to show towards certain holders of traditional dignities.

It was expected that the new Sultan would possess greater powers than his predecessor; for that alone would have provided him with authority. But instead of this, all temporal power was taken from him, and he was left with only spiritual power. He was like a judge without the power to sentence, a defender of the faith without a sword—and also with a foreign shield. It was repugnant to every Islamic conception.

A general uprising against the French administration threatened to break out. A year later the French government in Paris turned the rudder completely around, hastily deposed Ben ʿArafa, and let Mohammed V return from his exile in Madagascar. In December 1955, a purely Moroccan government was formed, to which, in the following March, France handed over all power. Morocco thus once again achieved its independence.

The political independence of Morocco, however, did not halt the spiritual decline, but on the contrary speeded it up. A state cannot be independent today without possessing the technical means which were invented in Europe. The adoption of these means involves an alteration in all the forms of the civilization in question; and if traditional forms are altered, they no longer retain the spiritual content which they previously possessed. In a genuine culture, which has its origin in a revealed religion, there is virtually no outward form, the loss of which would be without significance; all traditional forms, from law and morality to the art of the craftsman, are of such a nature that they can lead, from outward to inward, to the eternal meaning of life. The one who knows this meaning most profoundly—the saint or the sage—can dispense with outward forms; the collectivity cannot. For this reason the breakdown of the traditional forms of civilization in present-day Morocco is much more devastating than it ever was in Europe, because it has occurred so suddenly, and because the new has no relation whatsoever to the old, coming on the contrary from a foreign world.

The destruction, for instance, of the (apparently) most outward forms sometimes has the most far-reaching results. A cultured Moroccan said to me:

FAR RIGHT: *Along the Atlantic coast, at the westernmost limit of the Islamic world, a chain of simple domes mark the tombs of saints.*

'According to a French proverb, it is not the cloth that makes the monk, but one could just as rightly say that it *is* the cloth that makes the monk!' Indeed in most cases the disappearance of native Moroccan dress is the sign of a changed mental outlook. The pretext that European dress is more practical is only half true, and the wide Moroccan robes which freely envelop the limbs were much more suited to the North African climate with its considerable variability between hot and cold. At the same time, in their ascetical simplicity and virile patriarchal dignity, they express a certain spiritual bearing. The turban especially is like a sign of spiritual dignity, an expression, so to say, of the priestly role which was man's in the beginning; the Islamic tradition has ascribed this significance to it from remote times. It is the first thing to disappear, and is hotly opposed by modernists as the sign of backwardness.

European dress is fundamentally out of keeping with the postures and gestures of Islamic worship; it hinders bows and prostrations, renders the prescribed ablutions more difficult, and takes away the dignity of the effortless sitting together on the flat ground; whoever wears European clothes is either a 'gentleman' or a mere worker or 'proletarian'. Whereas previously men were differentiated only by their culture, the community is all of a sudden split into economically determined classes and, with the cheap products of the factory, a poverty without beauty invades the homes; ugly, senseless and comfortless poverty is the most widespread of all modern achievements.

Ibn Khaldūn says that the vanquished always tend to adopt the customs and practices of the victors, and so the victory-procession of Europe—not of France alone, or of any other European country as such, still less Western Christian culture, but of impersonal, technically omnipotent Europe—continues without a halt.

Islamic Moorish art, with the craftmanship which is basic to it, recedes before the machine; the town community is destroyed by the political press, and the cohesion of the nomadic tribes, as well as all genuine thinking is menaced by the radio. This irruption of the modern world does not resemble any historical change of earlier times; its incision cuts through everything. Only the vigilant consciousness of an inexpressible spiritual heritage can oppose it; and such a consciousness is in the nature of things rare.

I recently walked through the modern part of Fez with an elderly Moroccan friend, and wondered aloud about the warehouses which had been built there, and about the numerous machines which were on show. 'It is all inevitable,' said my friend, 'what must be, must be. And yet we had no need of any of it. For thirteen centuries we lived without all that, and we did not live badly. True, there were famines and wars, and sometimes also plagues; but we never had the worst of all plagues: unemployment.' 'And yet the young people admire all the novelties,' I said, 'and your young people who have been to Europe and studied there immediately renounce all that has been handed down to them.' 'That is because,' he replied, 'in your schools and universities the spiritual sciences have been displaced in favour of worldly "sciences".' 'And what happens when the "golden chain" (of tradition) is broken?' I asked. 'It will never be completely broken,' he said simply, 'but will continue in secret. There are times when the Spirit reveals itself, and times when it is veiled. But whatever happens, it will not happen without the will of God!'

We walked out of the town, past modern warehouses, past miserable shanties made of bits of wood and tin-cans and past tents and saints' tombs, until we reached the river Sabū, whose rushing earth-brown water flowed through an extensive marshland. A stone bridge with several arches traversed the river and the marshes. On the far side lay gentle hillsides, that were already enshrouded in the evening twilight. A few camp-fires glimmered in the distance. White birds—ibis—flew towards the town. The crescent moon had just risen. The ground quivered with the chirruping of insects. The whole earth quivered, and the air swirled up towards the sky. On the breakwater that supported the central pillar of the bridge, a fisherman knelt beside his line and prayed. He prostrated himself towards the south-east, touching the ground with his forehead.

The bridge had been built several hundred years previously by the ʿAlawite sultan Mulay Rashīd. It is big and strong, made of hewn stones, and put together without mortar. Over the years it had withstood the most violent floods. My friend walked back and forwards on top of it, pensively stroking its ancient stones.

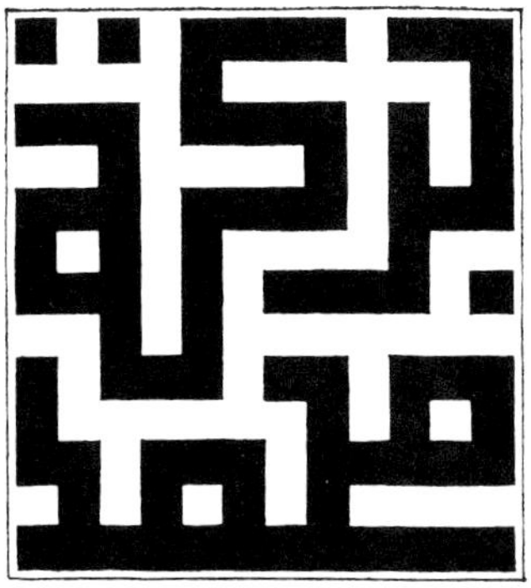

Afterword

Titus Burckhardt in Fez

TITUS BURCKHARDT'S monumental work, *Fez, City of Islam* first appeared in German in 1960, in the series *Stätten des Geistes* (Citadels of the Spirit), a series of which Burckhardt himself, on behalf of the Swiss publishing firm Urs Graf, was the founder and director.[1]

I should like to recall some of the circumstances surrounding the writing of this book by an author whose exemplary but discreet—and therefore unrecognized—role as a UNESCO expert and adviser to the Moroccan government during the years 1972 to 1977 was central in organizing a world campaign for the preservation of the venerable Medina of Fez, recognized as the 'intellectual capital' of the Kingdom of Morocco.

While suffering from a painful illness and awaiting with patience and serenity the outcome that would be decided for him by the Lord of the Worlds, Titus Burckhardt, at the request of some of his friends, had agreed to dictate '*Quelques souvenirs*' relating to the youthful years which he spent in Morocco.

His account of his second visit to Morocco in 1933–4—he was then 25 years old—begins with these words:

> Seeking a spiritual master, I settled in Fez, where I divided my time between this search and the study of Arabic. After six months, however, I had reached a dead end: I had been able to contact only 'men of the outward', either from the university circle, or from amongst the madmen of the district, who were more or less considered to be saints by the people of the town.

Then follows an account of his meeting with the sage Hajj Muḥammad Bu

Shaʿara of Salé (see picture on page 145), with whom he stayed for some time until the latter recommended him to one of the foremost of the *ʿulamā* of Fez. Mulay ʿAlī ben Tayyib Darqāwī, who was also a spiritual master, and heir to the *baraka* of his forefather Mulay al-ʿArabī al-Darqāwī (d. 1823), who was the founder of the Shādhiliya-Darqāwā Sufi order. It was Mulay ʿAlī who completed Titus Burckhardt's education—in Arabic, theology and mystical doctrine, making him read and learn by heart many chapters of the Koran, as well as the versified treaty on dogma and ritual by Ibn ʿĀshir; also making him attend the courses in traditional science, which he himself and other savants gave at the Qarawiyyīn University, then situated in the mosque of the same name, in the centre of the Medina. Burckhardt writes:

> On the day that Mulay ʿAlī gave his lectures in the great mosque, a saddled and caparisoned mule was waiting for him at the door of the sanctuary to take him back home shortly before midday. As soon as he was in the saddle, he told me to grasp the tail of the animal which trotted up the steep lanes of the Medina at a remarkable pace. While passing through the Gerniz district, where the houses join one another above the street, I suddenly noticed that the height of the street was at the level of Mulay ʿAlī's neck, and that he thus ran the risk of being beheaded. To my astonishment, he nimbly leant over the saddle in a horizontal position, immediately regaining his upright position with all the suppleness and rapidity of a reed in the wind.
>
> His garments were always in an impeccable condition and bore witness to his rank as a scholar. I sometimes saw him, however, in the garb of the Sufis, wearing a patched cloak. On these occasions he was withdrawn within himself, and difficult of access. One day he said to me that this dress derived from the practice of the Prophet.
>
> He cultivated the virtue of patience and often repeated the Sufi proverb: 'Saints are like the earth: it does not return the stones thrown at it, but only offers us its flowers.'

Nevertheless, if the tall silhouette of this blond young man dressed in a *jellaba* and turban had become familiar to the shopkeepers and craftsmen of the bazaar, many of whom offered a friendly '*salām*' to 'Sidi Ibrāhīm' as he passed by their stalls, the presence in the Medina of this unusual student quickly came to the attention of the Protectorate authorities, who began to be concerned. For members of the French administration, it was unimaginable that someone, especially a foreigner, could so diligently attend the courses at the traditional university, for other than political motives. A Swiss intellectual and artist officially converted to Islam could only be the cause of trouble and in the pay of a foreign power hostile to France . . . Whence the decision, in the form of a court action, to make him leave Moroccan territory. Once back in Switzerland,

Burckhardt was only able to return to Morocco a quarter of a century later, after Morocco had regained its independence in 1956.

The first person he visited was Hajj Muḥammad Bu Shaʿara of Salé, to whom he was bound by a sentiment of filial affection that had never weakened. The two men travelled together to Fez, where, Mulay ʿAlī having died in the meanwhile, they visited his tomb, and some of the sanctuaries of the town, including the *zawiya* where lies buried the Sufi ʿAlī al-Jamal (d.1780), a master of the mystical path of the Darqāwa's founder. In this *zawiya*, near the bridge Bain al-Mudun which joins the two banks of the River Fez and the two oldest districts in the town—that of the Andalusians and that of the Kairuanis—the two companions meditated for a long time, seated on mats in the little courtyard in front of the sanctuary, where the ground, covered with tiled mosaics (*zellij*) in the form of niches, covers the earthly remains of several venerable members of the brotherhood.

It was at this time, in spring 1960, that Burckhardt put the final touches to his work on Fez which had long been in preparation. Later the same year he published it in his native German. Burckhardt was to become in 1972 (and for the following five years) the inspirer and promoter of the UNESCO programme for the preservation of the Medina of Fez. Nevertheless, since Burckhardt's portrait of this city as he knew it in the thirties is that of a 'human city'[2]—in other words, a city capable of responding to all the needs of man: physical, emotional and spiritual—this portrait has not become out-of-date. Even better, since it depicts an urban model which is that of the classical Islamic city, it is rich in instruction for whomsoever, amidst the often anarchic pressures and tendencies of modern development, may be involved in the preservation of the irreplaceable qualities of life that flourish in a traditional urban environment.

For three years, starting from 1968, a series of representations had been made through the Moroccan National Commission of UNESCO to such international organisations as might be capable of taking action, to draw their attention to the value of the cultural heritage of Morocco and the dangers threatening it. Then, towards the end of 1971, it was decided to send a mission to examine the problems involved in preserving both the traditional monuments and the traditional crafts. As soon as he knew the aims of the study and the mandate of the experts—in which the preservation of the Medina of Fez figured highly—Burckhardt consented to collaborate, in the spirit of a doctor called to the bedside of a patient. In September 1972, we left together for Morocco.

Once there, our first task, in co-operation with the Ministry of Cultural Affairs at Rabat, was to draw up a joint working schedule and to allot tasks in the various sectors in which our primary investigations were to be made. Given his profound knowledge of the town and its society, it was decided that Burckhardt, accompanied by his wife, should take up residence in Fez, in order to study in detail the problems from which the old city was suffering, and to decide how best to safeguard not only its monuments, but also its craftsmanship, its urban fabric, and its viability in general.

I should be attempting the impossible if I were to seek to cover several years of activity by a man whose speed of comprehension and concentration were astonishing. I shall therefore limit myself to two aspects to which Titus Burckhardt never ceased to devote much time, so convinced was he of their usefulness and value: his teaching activity, as writer and speaker, and his field work, as investigator and organizer. In each of these roles Titus Burckhardt excelled.

As a speaker, he showed himself to be an exceptional teacher. Thanks to his natural humility he could place himself within the reach of more modestly endowed men. Without ever stooping to over-simplification or popularization, he was able to present with clarity key ideas and fundamental notions, which he developed from several points of view with a kind of benevolent slowness which enabled his audience to grasp his meaning almost in spite of themselves. In just one hour of leisurely talking, interspersed with pauses that might ease the process of reflection and assimilation, he would keep to a few essential themes, illustrating each of them with a few particularly striking examples.

To illustrate this, let me sketch the outline of the lecture referred to above, in which, addressing an audience of Fez residents, Burckhardt analysed what it was that gave Fez its character as a 'human city', something that had become quite exceptional in 'a world more and more mechanized, levelled and dehumanized'. He began by expressing his intuitive and convincing vision of the basis of Muslim 'civilization' (this word, derived from *civitas*, being viewed etymologically), which gives the Islamic city its particular value: 'The way of life, of which Fez is the crystallization, answers the needs of the whole man, who is at once body, soul and spirit, who has physical needs, an affective life of the soul, and an intelligence which transcends both of these planes . . .' From this primary insight there followed quite naturally a complete overview and explanation of the city: there was mention of the important role played by water (Fez is built on a watercourse, with tributaries and underground springs), an element essential for material life, aesthetic pleasure and ritual purification; there was mention of its characteristically 'inward-looking' architecture, so well suited not only to climate and social needs, but also to a fundamentally unitary religious perspective; there was mention of its 'dramatic' streets and alleys, 'sometimes narrow, sometimes wide, with many twists and turns like the passage-ways that guard the entrance to private houses—through wisdom and prudence, Fez never gave away her heart too easily'; and, finally, there was mention of its arts and crafts which, while meeting immediate physical needs, impart aesthetic pleasure and invite the soul to silent contemplation. 'It is in the nature of art to rejoice the soul, but not every art possesses a spiritual dimension. In the case of Moroccan art, this dimension is manifested directly by its intellectual transparency, by the fact that, with its geometrical and rhythmical harmony, this art is addressed, not to some particular intelligence characterized to a greater or lesser degree by passional tendencies but to intelligence as such, in its universal nature.'

Important as these considerations undoubtedly were for understanding the normative role of the Islamic city and for justifying the vast effort of preservation and restoration that had become necessary, it was never Titus Burckhardt's intention that they should remain merely theoretical. In his eminently practical fashion he set about putting them into practice with outstanding professional efficacy and competence. How, having defined and described them, was one to conserve and rehabilitate the permanent values of the city: its water resources, its architecture, its social fabric, its intellectual and artistic life?

It did not take Titus Burckhardt long to realize that no strategy could succeed without an inventory of the architectural heritage. This had never been done before, and he embarked on this task alone. Every morning he went down to the Medina with his drawing board and camera. He would seek out the leading men of the district and, with their help, would contact the owners of the large middle-class houses, who would then show him around these houses, while he began an inventory, made sketches and took photographs. In this way, an album describing some seventy beautiful Fez houses was prepared, followed by a similar inventory of sanctuaries great and small: mosques, mausoleums, and *zawiyas*. Each of these was labelled, and notes were made regarding its artistic importance and state of preservation. This essential field work, continued and completed by members of the interdisciplinary team of the Fez Master Plan, later formed the basis of numerous reports, generally anonymous, which eventually found their final home in the voluminous 'Master Plan for Fez' published in 1980.[3]

In artistic matters Titus Burckhardt's judgement and taste were infallible. He was devoted to Moroccan crafts, being well aware of their importance in fashioning a framework that reflected spiritual values, and he counted many craftsmen amongst his friends. Nothing escaped his notice as he walked through the Medina: not only the works of quality, both ancient and contemporary, that were offered for sale in the *sūqs*, but also the hybrid productions, often made by semi-industrial methods, that were bought by unwary tourists in the belief that they were objects of authentic craftsmanship. With unfailing courtesy, he would express to sellers of the former his admiration and encouragement, while to sellers of the latter, he would subtly indicate his reservations about the worth of objects that could tarnish the reputation of Moroccan craftsmanship.

In a programme designed to support the teaching of the traditional arts (drawn up at the request of the Ministry of Cultural Affairs), Titus Burckhardt, with his customary insight and concision, stressed the need to formalize and maintain artisanal teaching, as well as the cardinal importance of apprenticeship in the disciplines concerned:

> It must never be forgotten that the chief aim of the proposed schools is to restore a craftsmanship which has already fallen into decadence. The only way to halt this fatal trend is to set up strict training procedures, whereby master craftsmen, imbued with the purest traditional techniques, can integrally transmit to their apprentices both the form and the spirit of their craft . . .
>
> Schools of traditional arts and crafts must never be allowed to become refuges for pupils not gifted enough to study at ordinary schools. On the contrary, the schools of traditional craftsmanship must attract an élite in the area of visual talent . . .
>
> The importance of calligraphy does not merely reside in the fact that Maghribi ornamentation includes epigraphy: Arabic calligraphy, with its synthesis of rhythm and form, is, as it were, the key to all Islamic art, as well as the touchstone for the mastering of its style . . .
>
> As for the geometry of regular figures, this is the basis of the decorative arts of the Maghrib. The pupil must know how to construct these figures with the help of a ruler and compass; he must know how to develop one figure from another, and understand the laws of proportion inherent therein.
>
> The teaching of art history must be essentially visual; in other words, its aim is not to load pupils' memories with dates and technical terms, but to nourish their visual imagination. Without being exclusive, art history—or 'art typology'—must concentrate on Islamic art, the many variants of which contain essential lessons for students. For instance, could there be anything more important for an apprentice learning the art of *zellij* than the study of the enamelled terracotta decorations of the sanctuaries of Bukhara and Samarkand?

So far these recommendations have not been followed by concrete results. Expressed in different ways and on different occasions, they nevertheless underlie the entire philosophy of the preservation and rehabilitation programme which Titus Burckhardt, acting alone, pioneered for more than two years. He also remained the cultural adviser after the setting-up of the Master Plan Workshop for the preservation of the Medina and the future development of the city as a whole.

When this plan was completed at the end of 1977, Titus Burckhardt quietly returned to his home overlooking the Lake of Geneva. He came back to Fez in April 1978 to give a public lecture entitled 'Fez and the Arts of Islam'[4] in which he described the sanctuaries of Fez, their typology and architectural features, to a group of young civil servants from local government whose job it soon would be to interest the public in conservation measures.

A year later, also in Fez, he participated in a seminar organized by the then Committee for the Aga Khan Award for Islamic Architecture—he was a member of the grand jury—on the subject of 'Architecture as Symbol and Self-Identity'. In the course of the discussions, Titus Burckhardt intervened several times to emphasize and defend the central and symbolic role of Islamic Art.[5] On 9 April 1980 he went to Fez for the last time as guest of honour at the ceremonies organized by the Director-General of UNESCO to inaugurate a world campaign for the preservation of Fez.

Today Fez still remains the same seriously over-populated metropolis, with the same outworn infrastructure, which Titus Burckhardt wished to rejuvenate by enabling it to become once more the vehicle of essential and beautiful Islamic values which it could pass on to future generations. Nevertheless, Fez is a city where many miracles have already occurred and where, one day, the profound and truly realistic ideas and conceptions sown by Titus Burckhardt may still germinate and burst into flower.

Jean-Louis Michon
Chambésy
Geneva
1991

NOTES

[1] Besides the present volume, two other titles by Titus Burckhardt in this series, have been translated into English. These are: *Siena, City of the Virgin* (Oxford University Press, 1960) and *Chartres and the Birth of the Cathedral* (in preparation).

[2] *'Fès, une ville humaine'* was the title of a lecture given by Titus Burckhardt in the palace of the Pasha of Fez on 21 April 1973, to members of the Association for the Preservation of Fez, which had just been founded. This lecture was later published in *Etudes Traditionelles* (Paris), July-September 1984. See also 'Fez' in *The Islamic City*, UNESCO, Paris, November 1978.

[3] *Schéma directeur d'urbanisme de la ville de Fès*, UNESCO, Paris 1980.

[4] Published in *Actes du Séminaire expérimental d'animation culturelle*, Fez, 7 March to 28 April 1978, Fonds international pour la Promotion de la Culture, UNESCO, *Conférences*, volume 1, pages 109–119.

[5] See: *Architecture as Symbol and Self-Identity*, Proceedings of Seminar 4 in the series 'Architectural Transformations in the Islamic World', Fez, Morocco, 9 to 12 October 1979, The Aga Khan Awards, 1980.

List of Sources Quoted

AUTHOR	WORK	ABBREVIATION IN TEXT
^{c}Abd al-Ḥamīd Ḥamidū	*As-Sa^{c}ādat al-abadīya li-Abī Madyan Shu^{c}aib*, Tlemsen, 1304/1930	Ḥamidū
^{c}Abd al-Qādir al-Jazā'irī	*Qaṣīda*	^{c}Abd al-Qādir
^{c}Abd al-Karīm al-Jīlī	*Al-Insān al-Kāmil*	Al-Jīlī
^{c}Abd as-Salām ibn Mashīsh	*Ṣalāt*	Ibn Mashīsh
Abu'l-Ḥasan ^{c}Alī al-Jaznawī	*Zahrat al-Ās*	Zahrat al-Ās
Abū Madyan Shu^{c}aib	*Dīwān*	Abū Madyan
Adelhard of Bath		Adelhard of Bath
Al-^{c}Arabī ad-Darqāwī	*Rasā'il*	Rasā'il
Charmes, Gabriel	*Une Ambassade au Maroc*, 1886	Charmes
de Amicis, Edmondo	*Marocco*, Milan, 1886	de Amicis
de Amicis, Edmondo	*De la Dynastie Saadienne*, Bibliothèque Nationale, Paris, MS 5429, translated by E. Fagnan in *Extraits inédits relatifs au Maghrib*, Algiers, 1924.	Fagnan
Ibn Abī Zar	*Rawḍ al-Qirṭās*	Rawḍ al-Qirṭās
Ibn Khaldūn	*Muqaddima*	Muqaddima
Ibn Rushd (Averroes)	*Faṣl al-Maqāl*	Averroes
Ibn Tūmart	*Tawḥīd*	Ibn Tūmart
Leo Africanus		Leo Africanus
Loti, Pierre	*Au Maroc*	Pierre Loti
Lyautey, Maréchal	*Paroles d'Action*, Paris, 1927.	Paroles d'Action
Muḥammad al-Ḥarrāq	*Dīwān*	Dīwān al-Ḥarrāq
Muḥammad ibn Ja^{c}far al-Kattānī	*Salwāt al-Anfās*	Salwāt al-Anfās
Muḥammad Ẓāfir al-Madanī	*Al-Anwār al-Qudusīya fī Ṭarīq ash-Shādhiliya*	al-Madanī
Muḥyi'd-dīn ibn ^{c}Arabī	*Fuṣūs al-Ḥikam*	Fuṣūs
Muḥyi'd-dīn ibn ^{c}Arabī	*Rūḥ al-Quds fī munāṣaḥāt al-nafs*	Rūḥ al-Quds
Terrasse, Henri	*Histoire du Maroc*, Casablanca, 1949	Terrasse

Index of proper names, place names, and Arabic and Berber expressions